Wicked
BRIDGEPORT

Wicked
BRIDGEPORT

MICHAEL J. BIELAWA

THE
History
PRESS

Published by The History Press
Charleston, SC 29403
www.historypress.net
Copyright © 2012 by Michael J. Bielawa
All rights reserved

Cover images, clockwise from upper left: Dutch Schultz, *courtesy of the Library of Congress, LC-USZ62-111442*; decapitated heads, *Frank Leslie's Illustrated Newspaper*, December 29, 1866, *Michael J. Bielawa Collection*; corpse rising from the grave, *courtesy of the Library of Congress, LC-USZ62-11916*; Dr. Nancy Guilford, *courtesy of the Connecticut State Library*; General John F. Hartranft and his staff featuring Assistant Surgeon George L. Porter, *courtesy of the Library of Congress, LC-DIG-cwpb-04199*. Background map, *courtesy of the Bridgeport Public Library, Bridgeport History Center*.
Back cover: Head of murder victim in a bucket of embalming fluid, *courtesy of the Connecticut State Library*.

First published 2012
Manufactured in the United States
ISBN 978.1.60949.379.0

Library of Congress Cataloging-in-Publication Data
Bielawa, Michael.
Wicked Bridgeport / Michael J. Bielawa.
p. cm.
Includes bibliographical references.
ISBN 978-1-60949-379-0
1. Bridgeport (Conn.)--History. 2. Murder--Connecticut--Bridgeport. 3. Criminals--Connecticut--Bridgeport--Biography. I. Title.
F104.B7B54 2012
974.6'9--dc23
2011047611

Notice: The information in this book is true and complete to the best of our knowledge. It is offered without guarantee on the part of the author or The History Press. The author and The History Press disclaim all liability in connection with the use of this book.

To ERS,
thanks for the map

Contents

Acknowledgements

A number of institutions and dedicated individuals helped make this book, and my years of research, a pleasurable experience. To paraphrase one of my favorite nineteenth-century writers, Cardinal Newman, "What is useful is good, and what is good is in the Bridgeport Public Library's third-floor History Center." Truly, a Bridgeport treasure. I also want to thank Sara Santos in her Interlibrary Loan cubicle at BPL and librarians Jane Flynn for sharing your family stories about iron mining in the Berkshires and Nancy Sweeney for editorial suggestions.

The Connecticut State Library's History and Genealogy rooms are a home away from home. My family there includes Kevin Johnson (who is readily recognizable by the sounds of his clanging mess kit attached to his 29th Connecticut Colored Regiment uniform) and especially State Librarian Kendall F. Wiggin for his assistance (and offering to act as agent for my speaking tour).

Gregg Dancho, director of Connecticut's Beardsley Zoo, thanks for your years of friendship and support. I appreciate the safari survival tips. Bridgeport's past wouldn't be remembered without the forward vision of Kathy Maher, executive director and curator of the Barnum Museum, and Adrienne Saint Pierre's inspired approach to history is captivating. Thanks for your friendship and sharing your institution's marvelous collection.

Lesley Schoenfeld of the Historical and Special Collections, Harvard Law School Library, Cambridge; Gail Wiese, assistant archivist at Norwich University Archives and Special Collections, Kreitzberg Library, Northfield,

Vermont; the Abraham Lincoln Presidential Library and Museum, Springfield, Illinois; the Providence Public Library, Providence, Rhode Island; Linda Hocking, curator at the Helga J. Ingraham Memorial Library, of the Litchfield Historical Society, Litchfield, Connecticut; the Mason Library, Great Barrington, Massachusetts; and the Library of Congress Prints and Photographs Division have each made this work a greater reality. Kevin Morrissey of Stratford Town Hall's Engineering Department, once again you've hit the ball outta the park. It was a special honor working with Harry Colvocoresses, the great-great-grandson of Captain George Colvocoresses. Completing the mystic circle, the Bridgeport Community Historical Society deserves recognition for preserving the Park City's glorious story.

Manuscripts and coffee (and bourbon) were meant to go together. Ralph 'n' Rich's, Amici Miei, Take Time Café and Tiago's (with its haunted table) provided inspirational locales for turning pages of these drafts within the brick and gargoyle heart of old Bridgeport.

I'd like to thank my editors, Jeff Saraceno and Hilary McCullough, for their patience and guidance throughout the course of bringing *Wicked Bridgeport* to print.

My son Justin was a major influence hammering together *Wicked Bridgeport*'s introduction, and of course, this book would never have come to fruition without my wife Janice's sentiments and thought-filled touches. Thanks to everyone. See you downtown.

Introduction

Macabre stories of Hawthorne and Poe, Lovecraft and King have long populated fictional New England locales. Artistic temperament has always been inflamed by the region's rugged topography and weird history. Certainly this soil is fertile with stony legend. We've walked these dreamscapes; the crimes and sins entangling the alleys of Arkham, Massachusetts, and misty avenues in Castle Rock, Maine, provide a pathway to nightmare. Now another city can be added to this criminally haunted gazetteer: Bridgeport, Connecticut. It's all the more chilling considering that the bizarre tales lurking here are based on fact.

Dark places enjoy possessing New England. The region gathers peculiar worlds of shadowy woods, lonely country roads and, over the past half century or so, empty downtown streets. This is a realm known for whispering ghosts and beckoning waves. Bridgeport, too, embraces this mystique. The city has always been home to ship horns and train whistles, sounds that hold melodies of olden things.

Folded into New England's shoreline, Bridgeport Harbor opens onto Long Island Sound, once the haunt of pirates. The great wall of elevated railroad tracks running between Boston and Washington, D.C., cuts an ancient passage through town, but vanished rail lines a century ago followed a route beyond Bridgeport's northern reaches. These rails wended along the Pequonnock River, a waterway some attest is cursed. Shipping and trains assured industrial expansion. For decades, machines and manufacturing defined Bridgeport around the globe. Its munitions plants helped dub the city "the Essen of America." The smokestack industries have all left, but their presence still imbues the enduring brick and soot. Despite the vacuum of absent blast furnaces and row houses, factory barons and mill hands, Victorian legend and mystery remain. These primal totems, legend and mystery, wrestle for a hold over Bridgeport's shore and streets.

The foundation for my intrigue with local folklore was established early on. As I awoke from sleep, I felt my overnight bag being packed at the foot of my bed by Mom in my Yarmich Drive bedroom. Routinely, I hit the road with my grandparents, just about every weekend, driving throughout western Connecticut and the Berkshires, heading north to visit family in the Mohawk Valley. This was the 1960s. The imagined stories associated with all those tucked-away single–gas pump villages, crow-filled foggy morning roads and sun-dancing streams flowed into my psyche. But a lightning-rod moment occurred back in elementary school during fifth-grade clean-up, when students helped Mrs. Read arrange the room and put away books in preparation for glorious summer vacation. I discovered hidden in a cupboard an old collection of New England tales. One of the chapters featured a true-life treasure hunt by Boston-area author Edward Rowe Snow. Along with John Glenn, General Eisenhower, Ben Franklin and Abraham Lincoln, my list of childhood heroes immediately annexed Mr. Snow.

On an October night not too long afterward, freshly purple with leaves muttering among themselves (the perfect magic moment to uncover the incunabula of youth), I walked into the old Stratford Public Library and was awestruck to discover an entire shelf of Snow's haunting work. I have never left those New England mysteries. Later I delved wholeheartedly into the nineteenth-century writings of Samuel Adams Drake, the purveyor of Northeast legends and romance. I researched every pirate account along the Atlantic coast and read about every haunting taking place in New England. David Philips's *Legendary Connecticut* and Robert Ellis Cahill's voluminous work on strange events are still consulted cover to cover. Sir John Frazier's *Golden Bough* is always at hand.

Cable TV is nowadays chockfull of programs dedicated to exploring haunted houses, with whole crews charging into the woods scaring up mythic creatures or tackling psychic phenomena. They all owe a nod of gratitude to Drake and Snow. These two early protagonists of the uncanny certainly entertain as well as instruct. For over thirty years, I have walked in their candlelit footsteps, unearthing the strangely beautiful stories inhabiting New England. Since the mid-1970s, well before the above-mentioned camera teams traipsed through ghost-infested buildings, turning flat-screen TVs mossy-green with night-vision equipment, I have been a collector of legends. Researching throughout New England, and northward into the Adirondacks, I endeavored to preserve the paranormal. Closer to home, I was amazed at how the supernatural blended with Bridgeport's criminal past.

Yet all the while, it was puzzling to me how Drake and Snow could ignore one of the largest cities in New England. Perhaps the noisome proximity to bustling New York City? Or Bridgeport's over-the-top gritty, "bad boy" image may have misguided those in search of old New England. That's a crime. Farther afield, bloody deeds spawn scholarship. While Whitechapel's Jack the Ripper, New Orleans's Axe Man (and all his jazz) and, just down the road, Lizzie Borden all gather a romanticized following, Bridgeport's mysteries more often than not have remained savagely silent.

The truth is, Park City streets have cultivated ample precedent for the bizarre dating back to the Revolutionary era. An armchair survey of such antiquated tragedy allows readers a glance, through the safety of time, into the unvarnished past. Headline-grabbing crimes, especially unsolved cases, inherit an element of attraction. Reexamining these events offers the view of a particular cultural stage. This search for answers regarding the unexplained and unsolved combines historical fact with horror, cinching together a truer atmospheric New England chime.

One might not appreciate it from turning the pages of Drake and Snow, but the byways crisscrossing Bridgeport do hold weird "things." Sometimes these roads of legend are tangible. Blood-red milestones along this itinerary include secret societies, strange murders, pirates and bandits, as well as scientific attempts to raise the dead. These midnight tales take into account a New England border realm where truth and legend collide. Culled from a variety of sources, local histories, newspaper accounts and personal interviews, these stories have been harvested over many years. Evidence outlined here brings to light the fascinating heritage of a post-industrial New England city. The pilgrimage leads initiated travelers to the sound of a very different, moon-shadow drummer. Let Bridgeport's ship horns and train whistles act as your guide. You're invited to open this book and unfold its roadmap, but cautiously; things tripped upon along the way may not be uneven cobblestones underfoot. I wish you all a pleasant journey.

Buried in Bridgeport

1699–present

In the early settlement of the Colony of Connecticut, it was a place of resort and covert for pirates.
—R.R. Hinman, secretary of the state of Connecticut, 1836

Of all the villains who brazenly strode upon Bridgeport's shores, perhaps the most famous are those bloodthirsty pirates who, according to legend, knew this inlet at the mouth of the Pequonnock. Bridgeport owns a special place in pirate lore. What other New England community can lay claim to reveling so heartily in buccaneers that residents once erected a towering monument to the memory of Captain William Kidd, a man hanged for piracy and murder?

New England villages, so very far from turquoise bays and palm trees, launched an ungodly host of freebooters. Mean-spirited sea thieves left home to turn pirate or, as their brethren sportingly christened it, "go on account." Seamen from our region who inked their names to the abhorrent "articles" include some of the pirate round's most staggering characters. Off the coast of Maine, "the dread pirate" Dixey Bull was New England's first ocean raider; moving southward, the infamous Quelch held court at Marblehead; the maniacal Ned Low (who enjoyed slicing off his victims' lips, frying them and then forcing prisoners to eat the flesh) called Boston home; and Tew, hailing from neighboring Rhode Island, plundered Arabian and Indian ships of the Red Sea.

The waters of Long Island Sound were not devoid of this scourge. Sea-roving bandits were so numerous here that colonial records from early 1699 have Connecticut governor John Winthrop demanding a cessation of aiding and secreting pirates, "strictly charging and requiring that all pyrates seized within this Colonie with their goods and effects be sent into England under safe custody."

About the same time that Winthrop made his pronouncement, one of history's most infamous pirates, Captain William Kidd, was anxiously sailing north from the West Indies. Kidd was returning to his home port of New York, where he hoped to clear his name of piracy.

It is this legacy of Kidd and his treasure that still paces Bridgeport's shore. Was Captain Kidd familiar with the area? Assuredly. The seafarer from lower Manhattan knew Long Island Sound; he had friends in Connecticut and across the way on Long Island. Too smart to head directly into New York Harbor and risk arrest, Kidd sailed around Long Island on the Atlantic side. He entered the sound from the east during the first week of June 1699. Anchoring off Oyster Bay, an aloof twenty-five miles from his home, Kidd got word to his wife and attorney. The "obnoxious pirate" then lingered in Long Island Sound for several days, plying the waters off the beaches that would one day become Bridgeport.

Buried treasure offers a murky facet to the Kidd story. Intriguingly, before entering Boston on July 1 to discuss a pardon from the colonial governor (the plan failed, and a week later, Kidd was in chains), the accused pirate anchored off Block Island. Here, after a three-year absence, Kidd embraced his beloved Sarah. Mrs. Kidd was escorted by Thomas "Whisking" Clarke, an old family friend and a well-known smuggler who conducted business from a secret storehouse located in Stamford, Connecticut. Aside from Whisking Clarke, it is reported that various sloops visited Kidd at this time, perhaps transferring precious cargo to other friends for safekeeping. It is absolute fact that Kidd did indeed hide booty on neighboring Gardiners Island, a form of insurance awaiting his return from Massachusetts. These valuables were removed and inventoried by the authorities after the pirate was apprehended.

The Gardiners Island trove is an exception to piratical tendencies. Except for Captain Kidd, very few buccaneers actually buried treasure. Depraved crews were much keener on throwing ill-gotten gold at the requisite tavern pleasures. However, while incarcerated in Boston, Kidd was harangued by his jailer whether the prisoner would divulge the location of his hidden booty. Proving that some of his wealth was truly secreted, Kidd spat, "Nobody could find it but himself." This alluring hint was repeated just about two years later during his trial in London.

This 1894 artwork by Howard Pyle portrays Captain William Kidd burying stolen loot on Gardiners Island in eastern Long Island Sound. Rumors surrounding Captain Kidd burying treasure in the Bridgeport vicinity began soon after the pirate's visit to these waters in 1699. *Courtesy of the Library of Congress, LC-USZ62-62855.*

A week before his execution, Kidd composed a letter to certain members of Parliament explaining that if he was allowed to sail, naturally under guard, he could lead supporters to a rich trove he'd hidden. Combining Kidd's gold- and silver-filled chest hidden in the sands with John Gardiner and these prison confessions, it was bound for rumors to sprout about pieces of eight lurking in coves up and down the entire Connecticut coast. Kidd's treasure was supposedly secured on Charles Island off Milford, on Branford's Thimble Islands (especially Money Island), Fisher Island, somewhere on the coast of Westport or New London, buried on Sheffield Island off Norwalk and even up the Connecticut River as far north as Clarke's Island in Northfield, Massachusetts. Nutmeg State locations far removed from Long Island Sound can also lay claim to the pirate's treasure.

Following Kidd's hanging on Execution Dock at Wapping on May 23, 1701, his body was bound, tarred and gibbeted—that is, placed inside metal bands conforming to his body. This public exhibition warned others from embarking on a life of piracy. *Courtesy of the Library of Congress, LC-USZ62-86665.*

Connecticut's northwest corner has a Kidd connection in the form of a haunted house in Litchfield County's largest city. It is claimed that members of Kidd's crew escaped to Torrington with a share of the spoils. Nothing, as of yet, has been uncovered at any of these sites, although a sandbar off the Thimbles did yield a ring purportedly dating from 1610.

If tales be true, however, then Bridgeport, Black Rock and the Lordship section of Stratford could be the resting place of the riches Kidd alluded to in his gallows-bred confession. Treasure hunters have actively pored over this tidal triumvirate for more than 150 years. Some claim these investigations unearthed artifacts and precious objects, but in each instance, those lucky

Bridgeport's treasure island, Pleasure Beach, was home to a statue of Captain Kidd, as indicated on this 1896 map. Dedicated two years earlier, the granite pirate supposedly stood on the exact spot where Kidd hid his gold. *Map from* Atlas of the City of Bridgeport, Connecticut *(Philadelphia: D.L. Miller & Company, 1896); Michael J. Bielawa Collection.*

individuals associated with recovering coins and jewels have always, conveniently, vanished with the evidence.*

Perhaps the most precious treasure is the cache of pirate stories looming in the folds of Park City legend. In an effort to preserve these tales and assist archaeological research, here are the locations and strange strategies employed over the decades to recover local pirate booty; hopefully, these Bridgeport chanteys will aid some fortunate beachcomber net a glittering portion of the captain's long-lost wealth.

⚜ Much to the chagrin of those nineteenth-century adventurers infected with the gold bug, buried treasure traditionally demanded specific interaction with New England's invisible world. This was the case with what might be the earliest large-scale search for pirate treasure in the Bridgeport area. During the summer of 1851, a gathering of fifty to one hundred Spiritualists—the majority of whom reportedly resided in Bridgeport, Huntington and the Sandy Hook hamlet of Newtown, Connecticut—assembled with their wives and families about half a mile from the Stratford Point Light House for what historians have ever since referred to as the "Gold Diggings." From this factual event, future commentators assumed that the treasure's source was none other than William Kidd, but the Spiritualists were certain that they were on the verge of dislodging an unnamed Spanish pirate's booty, pilfered from the Bank of England with an estimated worth of somewhere between $7 and $10 million. Directions to the exact spot and the sorcery required to safely extract the treasure were detailed by an Albany clairvoyant. A quarter acre of land was acquired, and excavation began. To ensure secrecy, the work area was enclosed to avert the prying eyes of nonbelievers. A nearby bilge pump, once employed aboard an old Spanish privateer and later purchased by Stratford's Captain Samuel C. Nicoll for use at his Lordship manor, was used to suction the salt water out from the thirty-foot-deep

---

* During an October 28, 1982 interview with Stratford historian Franz Goldbach (1916–1991), he explained to the author that about the year 1925, farmer-trapper and avid Indian relic collector Anson Dart (1863–1933) shared with Goldbach and other Stratford children the location of a "pirate fort" on the shores of Long Island Sound. Looking back on his adventures with the amateur archaeologist, Goldbach explained, "The large cut stones they saw [on Prospect Drive] in Lordship, just below the rise [where the road intersects with Riverdale], running toward the bluffs, were the remnants of an ancient pirate fort. Dart brought out a cigar box full of old coins that were hexagon-shaped, and he called them his pieces of eight." Dart impressed upon Goldbach and the other children, "If you want some of your own pieces of eight, you should dig around the old pirate fort."

"Spiritual Hole." The medium demanded silence be maintained at all times throughout the strenuous two-hours-a-day regimen; visitors to the diggings remarked how the assembled ghost worshipers appeared mute in that they communicated only through hand gestures. Curious townspeople heading to the beach peered down from the bluff to observe the Spiritualists glide in silent procession, often flowing into a séance ring in the sands. The diggers energetically stated that one ironbound chest was actually struck with a tool but sank into the earth. The story goes that the excavation continued unabated for nearly a month until, on the thirtieth day, someone's foot was painfully struck by a spade. The piercing yelp broke the clairvoyant's spell, and as the magic dispersed, the Spiritualists felt forced to abandon the dig.

❧ Minus the shuddering hand of the supernatural, treasure was apparently discovered just two miles north of downtown Bridgeport. According to the *New York Times*, during the winter of 1884, Italian gandy dancers working to clear the Olmstead Railroad extension at the head of the Pequonnock River unwittingly found something quite out of the ordinary. One of the itinerant workers sunk his pickaxe into a crevice and, while yanking the heavy tool free, dislodged a silver-tipped powder horn. Closer examination of the ivory object found it resplendent with indecipherable "hieroglyphics." More astonishingly, rattling inside the horn were found several old English coins, a Spanish doubloon and a section of parchment. The discovery unsettled the railroad men, who, over the course of the next several nights, excitedly dug for additional precious antiquities. Neighbors heard the nocturnal activity and figured something peculiar was afoot, but the language barrier between the Italian immigrants and the Bridgeporters precluded any satisfactory explanation. It wasn't until a bout of heavy fog lifted that the extensive dig was exposed. The ground near the rail bed had yielded a cache of silver vessels, coins and an assortment of decayed sword hilts. The *Times* also alluded to the unearthing of an iron strongbox. Piqued by curiosity, the locals inspected the workers' camp, but it was too late; the railroad men had fled with their findings.

❧ In early 1887, Bridgeport resident Walter Nichols purchased Long Beach from the Town of Stratford with the intention of creating an amusement park. Near Point-No-Point, a foundation was dug for one of the park's buildings; this was the area familiar to the Spiritualists of 1851. A large earthen jug was discovered containing arrowheads and spear points, along with the bones of two children.

⚜ East Bridgeport resident Samuel Middlebrook, with a medium's assistance, acquired a sacred divining rod, a Y-shaped stick imbued with the magical ability to detect hidden treasure. In early February 1889, the spirit-guided branch pointed a path to Fairfield Beach and then the next night directed the Brooks Street wagon driver to the buttress of Washington Bridge, near the mouth of the Housatonic. A crew was hired at a cost to the treasure hunter and both areas were excavated, but nothing was found.

⚜ Record-setting storms during July and August 1889 helped intensify the search for treasure on Long Beach. The Stratford Land Improvement Company had been building a levy along the barren three-mile stretch between Pleasure Beach and Lordship to help insulate the marsh entrance known as the Gut. Torrential rains chiseled countless rivulets leading from the sandy berm down to the Sound's edge when someone plucked a glittering flicker from one of the gullies. It turned out to be an English coin. Soon, a handful of old gold and silver currency, supposedly dating back two hundred years, surfaced.

⚜ Once again, the unseen hand contorting a dowsing rod grasped the heart of a Park City resident. John Hall's twenty-year search for Kidd's booty, through the use of a mystic branch, came to a snapping halt during the autumn of 1893. The eighty-five-year-old prospector's incessant claims of magic finally compelled his distraught sons to file papers for their father's institutionalization.

⚜ An amusement park on Pleasure Beach was finally realized in 1892 by liquor entrepreneurs J.H. McMahon and P.W. Wren. Two years later, James Sexton & Son, who made their living carving headstones and monuments at their Crescent Avenue stoneworks, were given a peculiar commission. They were asked to construct a granite Captain Kidd. The twenty-five-foot-tall monument was ferried under wraps to Pleasure Beach during mid-June 1894. Plans called to erect the statue on the exact spot where tradition held that the pirate and his crew buried their treasure. Bringing joy to pirates and anarchists everywhere, the unveiling took place during the park's 1894 Fourth of July festivities.

⚜ Curtis Dart and William Hodge were counted among Bridgeport's best-known gentlemen of leisure. These happy-go-lucky hoboes had wended through life collecting suntans and surviving on the clams they dug. Profits raked in during low tide were distributed evenly among the many Water Street saloons. All was right among the spittoon and foot-rail denizens of the city's harbor-front taverns until one October evening in 1894, when a barkeep noted aloud how Dart's and Hodge's elbows were missing from his gaslit establishment. The whiskey-toting regulars slowly returned their glasses to the stained mahogany and glanced around the smoky room. There'd been a serious storm just the other day; a rogue wave or violent undertow could have easily swept their drinking buddies out to sea. Inquiries proved fruitless. Hodge and Dart were gone.

A year later, Water Street became abuzz when the two missing clam diggers suddenly threw open the doors to their old swilling haunts. Mugs and tumblers paused at parched lips and eyebrows arched; not only were the old shabby fellows alive and well, but they were surprisingly well heeled. Hodge and Dart had somehow, shockingly, been transformed into diamond-wearing gentry. Rounds of strong drink proffered by the pair crossed many bars along the waterfront thoroughfare that engaging day, producing hooting backslaps and, more importantly, harvests of gossip. While paying for ale, one of the dandy's pockets exposed a collection of jewel-encrusted gold. Loose lips from one of the wealthy barflies divulged Captain Kidd's name. A hasty explanation brought to light a tale of treasure found on Stratford's Point-No-Point being exchanged in New York for stocks, real estate and Manhattan lodgings. Ever afterward, the grog quaffers of Water Street reasoned that Kidd's booty was the only possible method these perpetual beach wanderers could have become prosperous in so quick a fashion.

⚜ A few days shy of the April 21, 1898 American blockade of Cuba, the final precursor to hostilities igniting the Spanish-American War, an army of Bridgeport munitions workers marched on Pleasure Beach. A handful of Spanish coins, dated 1731, were unearthed in a trench, thus prompting the shovel and pick brigade. About this same time, Walter Nichols, who had owned Pleasure Beach, invited two representatives from an English munitions manufacturer to stay at his Courtland Street home while they conducted business in Bridgeport. Nichols immediately regretted his decision. The emissaries, who were Spanish, began whispering about the war and were acting strangely. Neighbors

The Captain Kidd monument stood twenty-five feet tall and greeted Pleasure Beach visitors as they disembarked from the island's ferry. By 1914, the statue had toppled over and was surrounded with trash. *Courtesy Connecticut State Library.*

were relieved when one day the pair vanished from town. Soon after, during a hike on Pleasure Beach, Nichols ran across a deep hole. Around the lip of the crater, several Spanish gold coins were scattered in the sand. It was Walter Nichols's contention that his house guests had somehow become alerted to Kidd's treasure and, under the guise of munitions contractors, remained in the city until they secured and removed the booty.

Hopefully, treasure seekers will always search for Kidd's legendary loot and, with their shovels and dreams, augment the chapters of local folklore. But a very real treasure lurking on Pleasure Beach has been thoroughly ignored: the Captain Kidd statue lost to the sands of this peninsula. As of 1914, the neglected monument had capsized, and the pirate chieftain was disrespectfully left reclining among the flotsam and jetsam of tin cans and driftwood. An attempt to right the granite figure and pedestal took place in 1916, but the now armless monument listed terribly to the captain's port side. Disgraced with graffiti and weather beaten, the statue was mockingly reduced to a joke. What eventually happened to Bridgeport's pirate sentinel remains a mystery. Perhaps one day, following an archaeological investigation, Captain William Kidd's visage will be unearthed, allowing him to set his stony eyes once again upon Bridgeport's shore.

The Curious Circumstances Surrounding the Demise of Captain Colvocoresses

1872

As with sacred places, so with the murderous spots—the record of events is written into the earth.
—*Henry Miller,* The Colossus of Maroussi

E very pathway holds a story. Maybe more so those cobblestone roads that have vanished. Take, for instance, Clinton Street, a shortcut leading from Main Street toward Bridgeport Harbor. In the 1870s, a home or two, a boardinghouse and a small shed lined its plank walkways. These structures once stood just a little south of today's Barnum Museum. Now Clinton Street lies buried below ground, somewhere beneath the shadows of the elevated portion of I-95. Sailors assuredly walked, and some undoubtedly stumbled, on this road to and from their ships docked beyond the railroad tracks. The footsteps of one sailor in particular have a tragic attachment to this lane. At night, the echoes of his footfalls can still be heard. Captain George Musalas Colvocoresses, a man famed for his exploration of the uncharted Pacific, took a journey down this short Bridgeport road from which he never returned. Naval histories chronicling his Clinton Street demise note it as one of the greatest unsolved mysteries of all time.

Colvocoresses's death matched the violence he'd witnessed as a child. George was born in 1816 into a prominent family on the Aegean island of Chios. In 1822, during the Greek War for Independence, Turks invaded the island, ravaging towns and decimating the population. Upward of sixty thousand inhabitants were slaughtered. Seeking refuge within the island's

George Musalas Colvocoresses (1816–1872) is pictured here during the Civil War. "Colvos" survived slavery, rugged expeditions and warfare—only to die in Bridgeport under circumstances navy histories label as one of the military's greatest mysteries. *Courtesy of Norwich University Archives, Kreitzberg Library, Northfield, Vermont.*

interior proved a false hope. As the Turks prepared to attack the hamlet where the Colvocoresses family was concealed, heeding his wife's tearful pleading, George's father, Constantine, escaped during the battle in order to work out a ransom. With the assistance of the Austrian Consulate, Constantine secured the freedom of his family. George, who had been enslaved, witnessed the execution of an uncle, and his grandmother was beaten to death before his eyes.

To ensure the six-year-old's safety, George, along with nine other boys, was placed on the American brig *Margarita* sailing for Baltimore. The plight of the ocean-borne orphans struck the hearts of everyone in America. George came to the attention of Captain Alden Partridge, who requested that the young refugee be sent to Vermont, where he'd be raised as a member of the family and educated in the military academy (later Norwich University) where Partridge was headmaster. George remained in Vermont ten years, studying and working the family farm. With the sponsorship of Partridge in 1832, the sixteen-year-old entered the U.S. Navy with the rank of midshipman.

After serving in the Mediterranean, George was promoted to passed midshipman and attached to the Wilkes Exploring Expedition. During this hair-raising duty, lasting from 1838 to 1842, Colvocoresses helped chart the Pacific and survey the coasts of three continents, from Alaska to Cape Horn, as well as the ice fields of Antarctica. In 1841, Colvocoresses took part in the overland portion of the expedition, traveling America's Northwest from Vancouver to San Francisco. The Wilkes crew surveyed 280 islands, created 180 charts and discovered two hundred new species. Due to Colvocoresses's able-bodied assistance, one of the Fiji Islands, a passage in Puget Sound and a bay off Antarctica are all named in his honor. Colvocoresses documented his adventures in *Four Years in a Government Exploring Expedition*, published in 1852.

During his subsequent naval career, Colvocoresses was stationed throughout the world. In 1843, he was promoted to lieutenant and was warmheartedly nicknamed "Colvos" and "Crawl-over-crosstrees" by tongue-tied tars. Three years later, while on leave in Vermont, he fell in love and married Eliza F. Halsey. Returning to duty, he served off the coasts of Africa and the Mediterranean for many years, during which time he nearly died from yellow fever. Wracked with the illness, Colvocoresses appeared as if he had expired, and his remains were prepared for burial at sea. While the chaplain performed the last rites, the American flag draped over George's body shuddered ever so slightly with his breath, and the lieutenant was saved from a watery grave. One permanent effect of the illness was Colvocoresses's loss of hair; for the rest of his life, he donned a wig.

In the late 1850s, Colvos served as executive officer of the sloop of war *Levant*, actively participating in the Battle of the Barrier Forts near Canton, China, at the onset of the Second Opium War. At the outbreak of the American Civil War, he was promoted to commander of the USS *Supply* and was at the mouth of the Mississippi River when New Orleans surrendered. While on this duty, in 1862, his first wife died, and the following year, he married Adeline Swasey, the younger sister of Captain Alden Partridge's wife. Placed as commander of the USS *Saratoga*, he joined the South Atlantic Blockading Squadron, during which time he carried out several successful intelligence-gathering raids along the Georgia shore. During these raids, Colvos liberated a number of slaves. Toward the end of the war, Colvocoresses was stationed off the west coast of South America. Upon returning from the Pacific in 1867, he was promoted to captain and retired.

For the first time in years, Colvocoresses returned to family life in Litchfield, Connecticut. Afterward, with hopes of financially supporting his family, the captain became embroiled with navy brass in an attempt to receive remuneration equal to that provided to other navy officers for service rendered and prizes captured.

Preparing for his case against the federal government necessitated frequent excursions away from home. During this time, he also began accumulating life insurance policies for the amount he thought the navy owed him. On Monday morning, June 3, 1872, the captain trimmed some fruit trees in his garden and front yard before bidding his wife an affectionate goodbye and departing his Litchfield home for a business appointment in New York City. He was delivering stocks and bonds to his insurance agent, Alfred Smith, for a premium deposit. In addition, the captain was reportedly carrying $8,000 in cash. At the Shepaug Valley Railroad stationhouse, he checked his valise in the baggage car and boarded the train to Hawleyville. From there, he would complete the trip to Bridgeport on the Housatonic Railroad. Colvos often visited the Park City and was familiar with the serpentine route of the new Shepaug line's two daily trains. Usually the captain was joined by special freight, the Borden's milk regularly transported from the company's condensery in Washington Depot.

Looking out the window as the steam engine wound through western Connecticut's little riverside towns and farmland, the captain tapped his bamboo cane to the rhythm of the clacking rails. This walking stick was a trusted companion, especially when traveling with valuables; within the bamboo scabbard, a sword was hidden. On a more conservative note, the career military man as usual planned ahead and brought an umbrella.

Arriving in Bridgeport, Colvos gathered his bag and immediately reported to the wharves near the Housatonic Railroad roundhouse, where the side-wheeler *Bridgeport* waited tethered to the Naugatuck Dock. After purchasing a ticket for New York and finding the stateroom to his liking, Colvos deposited his russet valise and walked down the plank toward Water Street carrying his cane-sword, umbrella and a small black Moroccan leather traveling satchel. He popped into one of his favorite haunts, the Sterling House hotel on Main Street, but was informed they had stopped serving dinner for the evening. It was 9:15 p.m. So the captain took a short walk around the corner to Bank Street for a bite at Ward's restaurant. After his visit to the eatery, Colvocoresses came back to the Sterling, pleasantly chatting out front with the host and a desk clerk. Colvos handed the proprietor a Sterling House room key he had forgotten to return from his stay at the hotel the previous week.

Noting the time, it was now half past ten (the steamship departed at eleven o'clock); he purchased a cigar, inquired about the most direct route to the dock and bid the gentlemen good night. Walking south along Main Street, the captain paused at M.H. Wheeler's drugstore for two sheets of writing paper and two envelopes, explaining that he'd like a smaller envelope able to fit inside the larger. The seaman asked once more for directions to the boat, so Mr. Wheeler walked the captain to the sidewalk and pointed the way. The store proprietor glanced at his watch; it was now 10:35 p.m. Except for his murderer, no one would see Captain Colvocoresses alive again.

For some unknown reason, Colvos turned left off Main when he came to Clinton Street instead of heading farther along to South Street as directed. Folks afterward thought he may have become confused during the late hour, but then again, the captain knew Bridgeport's streets. Some men chatted

The Sterling House Hotel (present-day Arcade Apartments) was built about 1840 and expanded in 1852. Captain Colvocoresses departed from these front doors and walked south on Main Street, where he tragically met his end a few blocks away. *Courtesy of Nancy Sweeney.*

quietly on the northwest corner of Main and Clinton. A woman came down Main and suddenly broke into a run across Clinton, ran past a number of houses and then turned back and ducked into a brick dwelling. Church bells sounded, and the whistle of the departing steamer wailed; it was preciously eleven o'clock. Somewhere, the unmistakable report of a pistol joined the night's noises. Police officer L.M. Bailey, stationed at the docks whenever the New York–bound boat was in town, raced in the direction of the blast. Lying prone near a picket fence, the glowing victim was easy to locate in the dark. Flames from that portion of shirt covering his heart guided Bailey. Officer Hogan quickly joined him on Clinton Street; they found three other gentlemen there who'd also been summoned by the loud gunshot. Explorer and Civil War hero George Colvocoresses gasped two short breaths and died in a pool of blood and cinder.

The aftermath of the case generated a labyrinth of questions, particularly concerning what had transpired during the captain's final twenty-five minutes of life when the steamer *Bridgeport* was docked just an eight-minute walk from the druggist. Neighbors peering from their windows after the gunshot said they hadn't seen anyone leaving Clinton on the Main Street side, and Officer Bailey, approaching from Water Street, saw no one exiting from the opposite side. However, one resident reported hearing footsteps in his backyard.

After Colvocoresses's body was removed to the police station for an official inquest, authorities attempted to piece together the evidence. A single bullet had passed through the body, downward below the left breast and through the stomach, severing the spine and leaving a long exit wound in Colvos's right hip. The pistol had been placed directly against his chest, and the blast ignited his shirt.

The $8,000 in cash, his black satchel and watch were missing. His pockets revealed only $2.70 and the key to his stateroom aboard the side-wheeler (where he had left his valise). The gun used in the shooting was located diagonally across the street from the body, thirty to thirty-five feet away in the gutter. It was a "large clumsy horse pistol of ancient French manufacture." The wooden stock of the converted flintlock had broken apart from the barrel and lay a half dozen feet from the body. Closer inspection showed that the sections were fractured from an old crack and the pieces had been held together with glue and wrapped with tarred twine. The captain's constant companion, his secret sword, was considerably bent during the struggle; it lay unstained near the gutter, about two yards from his feet. Next to the splintered bamboo cane sheath was his umbrella.

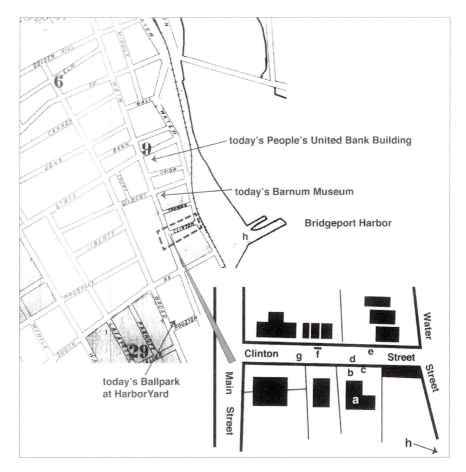

Downtown Bridgeport, Clinton Street; site of Captain George M. Colvocoresses's mysterious death, June 3, 1872. **a.** house; **b.** captain's body; **c.** umbrella; **d.** broken bamboo cane/secret sheath; **e.** pistol; **f.** gutter plank where powder horn was found; **g.** red pillbox/percussion caps; **h.** leather satchel found on railroad tracks under rail car. *Composite image created by Michael and Janice Bielawa based on contemporary newspaper accounts and Bridgeport maps 1875, 1889.*

The following morning, June 4, 1872, Colvocoresses's black satchel was discovered farther down Water Street, about eight hundred feet from the body, beneath a train car near the wharf. It was empty except for a blank checkbook. The contents had been removed after the bag was slit open with a dull blade. A search of Clinton Street led to the discovery of a red pillbox holding percussion caps and a large-caliber bullet. They were all discovered tied in a rag some sixty feet from where the pistol lay. On June 5, word about the captain's extensive life insurance holdings began to circulate. The total came close to a staggering $200,000. A couple of days later, a boy saw a bit of cloth peeking from under a Clinton Street gutter plank; playfully yanking the soiled rag, he found it connected to a battered powder horn. Evidently, it had been tucked there by the killers for safekeeping.

Rumors blazed over Bridgeport like a sea-filled oil fire. Most believed the captain's death was an atrocious murder, but others were equally certain that it was Colvos's own plan to end his life. Others still thought this deed must have been an accomplice-aided suicide. Some postulated the captain faked his killing by hiring a down-and-out "substitute" so he could renew his life elsewhere—maybe return to the exotic Fijis of his younger navy days.

Bankers in Litchfield, meanwhile, discovered at least $15,000 in U.S. bonds absent from Colvocoresses's accounts. The missing funds began adding up. While searching the captain's private box, held by the First National Bank at Litchfield, a memorandum dated May 13, 1872, was discovered; it listed bonds destined for deposit totaling $80,000. Colvocoresses wrote, "Those [stocks] marked with the letter 'D' I shall, on my arrival in New York place in [the insurance company's] 'safe deposit.'"

The bonds listed with the initial D were not among the remaining papers in his bank box. It was presumed that they had been in the satchel Colvos carried with him to Bridgeport.

Reward offers sprouted: for leads pertaining to Colvocoresses's murderer(s), the captain's widow would provide $3,000; the governor of Connecticut, Marshall Jewell, offered $2,000; and Bridgeport Mayor Epaphras B. Goodsell offered another $2,000. An additional $10,000 was offered for the return of the bonds.

However, investigations led nowhere. The *New York Sun* assigned blame with local police, lambasting Bridgeport authorities for not thoroughly following up on "three suspicious men" seen on the corner of Main and Clinton just prior to

The official 1872 wanted poster offering a $5,000 reward for the apprehension of Captain George Colvocoresses's killer(s). *Courtesy of Harold L. Colvocoresses.*

the pistol shot. The newspaper questioned why there was no effort to chase after "two [other men who] were heard running away from the spot immediately after the shooting." The *New York Sun* also noted that the skipper of the *Bridgeport* had seen two "strangers" acting suspicious on the docks the evening before the murder. In addition, the *Sun*'s editors questioned the whereabouts of William Sanks (alias H.C. Jenks, alias Dr. Squills) and Alonzo Swords, two prisoners serving time for assault and robbery who had been released from the Bridgeport jail on the same day as Colvos's death.

Evidence was compromised and lost, too. The captain's pants, which allegedly showed rips from a struggle, were stolen from the stationhouse by a tramp. The tarred twine used to hold together the damaged pistol went missing, and Chief Rylands inadvertently tampered with evidence when he had the gun repaired. On the evening of Colvocoresses's death, sailors aboard a three-masted schooner in Bridgeport Harbor had been firing a pistol, reportedly to kill wharf rats. When police discovered the ship had left port the morning after the captain was shot, Chief Rylands requisitioned a boat and intercepted the craft. The *Sun*'s scribes shook their heads. Bridgeport officials never boarded the schooner but merely quizzed the craft's captain from afar.

Insurance companies protecting their investments aggressively drew the conclusion, however circumstantial, that Colvocoresses had strategized to kill himself. The executor of the Colvocoresses estate brought suit against the companies that, in turn, painted a damning picture. Alfred Smith, Colvocoresses's agent, happily provided testimony throughout the investigation on behalf of the insurance conglomerates. One of the most compelling mysteries surrounds Colvos's unaccounted-for final twenty-five minutes. The distance from the drugstore where Captain Colvocoresses spoke with the owner to the New York–bound boat was merely an eight-minute walk. The insurance companies expressed that the extra time was used to remove the pistol from the satchel, cut the bag open and hide it under the train, rush back to Clinton Street, prep the gun with gunpowder and ball, hide the powder horn and then shoot himself.

One witness, a woman living in the house in front of where the tragedy occurred, explained that she had both shutters wide open and a light in the room so bright she declared that it shone directly onto the street. While undressing for bed, she heard what she interpreted as a stick breaking and then, twenty or so minutes later, heard the gunshot. At that point, she was so frightened that she pulled the sheets over her head and did not go to the window for some time. Down the street, another witness ran to her window "in a few seconds" after the sound of the blast but saw no one; however, investigators noted that the view from her ground-floor room was blocked by shrubs and buildings.

As the trial approached, the insurance firms excruciatingly gathered facts that they felt proved beyond a doubt that Colvos had committed suicide. Most damaging of all was the insurance companies' exhaustive investigation that tracked down every owner of Connecticut Valley Railroad securities. The captain listed these stocks on the deposit memorandum found in his Litchfield bank. They were supposed to be part of Colvos's premium payment and the reason for his visit to New York. Investigators found that Colvocoresses did not, and never did, own a single share in this railroad company.

In the end, fearing a long and expensive trial, during which the jury could very likely side with a well-known dead hero, the majority of insurance companies settled out of court. In March 1874, they agreed to a 50 percent buyout on their policies, except for the New York Life Insurance Company, which honored its policy in full. The captain's heirs received somewhere in the amount of $102,000; after expenses and legacies were deducted, $77,000 was distributed among his family. In accordance with Colvocoresses's will, various charities received donations, including the Bible Society and the Society for the Relief of the Destitute Children of Seamen. An additional $1,000 was set aside to erect a monument in Vermont to be placed on the grave of his mentor, Captain Alden Partridge.

Still, a multitude of unanswered questions suggest that Colvocoresses was murdered. He had no reason to kill himself; he loved his family, appeared happy and was in good health (as proved by his life insurance physicals). Representatives from New York Life questioned other insurance investigators' claims that every share of Connecticut Valley Railroad stock had been tracked down and accounted for. Therefore, the company reasoned, Colvocoresses could have owned shares. After its own investigation, the company agreed with Robert Pinkerton, the famous detective, that the captain was indeed murdered.

Drawn from witness testimony, newspaper accounts, insurance reports and medical publications, many intriguing points prove the captain was slain:

⚜ Most puzzling is how did the weapon end up across the street, thirty to thirty-five feet from the body? Doctors noted it would be physically impossible for a person to shoot himself in such a manner and then throw the gun.

❧ Colvos purchased two sheets of paper and envelopes before he died. What did he write, and where did the sheets go?

❧ Fifteen minutes prior to the shooting, three men stood nearby; who were they?

❧ That summer's newspapers were full of reports of rowdies roaming downtown. Grocer John L. Wessells, future three-term mayor of Bridgeport, on his way to the side-wheeler reported that he saw two men standing in the shadows near a wooden shed on the south side of Clinton Street. As Wessels approached, he overheard one man whisper to the other, "He's not the one."

❧ Would a military man use such an old gun held together with glue and wire, which might misfire or merely wound?

❧ There were no powder burns on the captain's hands, as would be expected from a pistol blast.

❧ One has to question the validity of a witness who "heard" a noise like a stick breaking and later a gun blast. Her upstairs room was well lit; she remembers finite details, except for closing the curtains before undressing in front of an open, brightly illuminated window. Is her story trustworthy?

❧ Why did Albert Smith, the insurance agent, allow the purchase of so many policies? Was there a scam involved?

❧ At roughly four o'clock in the morning following the tragedy, an unidentified man entered the railroad switch house in New Haven, saying he'd walked from Bridgeport that night. With no chance to see a morning paper, he inquired about the Bridgeport murder when the day watchman came on duty. Told that there was extensive coverage about Colvocoresses being found dead, the stranger hastily left. The unknown, "respectable looking" man was last seen walking the rails toward Hartford.

Suspects would continue to appear. Like long-vanished Judge Crater or skyjacker D.B. Cooper, for decades the specter of Colvocoresses's mysterious demise reared its inky head in newspapers. The nationally known humorist for the *Danbury News*, James Montgomery Bailey, employed the unsolved case in an article debating a person's identity: "I didn't know if he was a theologian in the ecstasy of pin-feathering, or the murderer of Captain Colvocoresses, searching for a pinnacle on which to stand and curse his fate and count his plunder."

In 1873, eleven months after the captain's death, noted burglar Jim Brady was arrested in New York with a large amount of bonds in his possession. Authorities hinted that these were the securities Colvocoresses supposedly carried when he was shot.

Thirteen years after Colvocoresses's death, a truly sensational account spread across the country that supposedly resolved the case. Off the coast of the Hawaiian Islands, Danish sailor Baldwin Jansen became extremely ill. Possessing a sailor's superstitious disposition, he was unable to die without confessing a horrible sin and "sent for the [ship's Captain Donaldson] to come to the forecastle, saying 'that he had something on his mind.'"

The *New York World* described the deathbed confession. The Dane was often in port at Bridgeport, and he, along with other sailors, was accustomed to seeing Colvocoresses head toward the eleven o'clock boat for New York. He had heard that Colvos carried money in his handbag and was determined to rob him. He didn't intend to kill the captain, but…

> On the fatal night [Jansen] *followed* [Colvocoresses] *to the lonely portion of Clinton Street, ran up nimbly behind him and seized the coveted bag. Capt. Colvocoresses turned and struck Jansen with his sword-cane, and Jansen tried to wrench the bag away but Colvocoresses being a large man retained his clutch. The blows from the cane fell fast until it was broken, and Jansen, fearing Colvocoresses would thrust him with the protruding sword point, drew his pistol and fired. Colvocoresses dropped. Jansen ran across the street, dropped the pistol and bullets where they were found, cut open the bag with his sheath-knife, flung the bag under the [railroad] car, and escaped upon the schooner in the harbor. In wrenching the bag from Colvocoresses he forced the captain's seal ring from his hand. This he thrust into his pocket. Fearing detection from the officers who boarded the schooner, he threw the bonds overboard. The ring he secreted in one of the schooner's "knee" timbers and covered* [the jewelry] *with oakum and pitch.*

The Danish seaman handed Captain Donaldson the ring, making him promise to return it to its rightful heirs. Jansen died and was buried at sea off Honolulu in January 1885.

The tale, though well told and riveting, was branded by newspapers as a pack of lies. No one was more surprised to read the account than Baldwin Jansen, a chauffer who lived just five miles outside of Bridgeport. Of course, this begs the question that it was a different Baldwin Jansen who confessed and died in the Pacific Ocean, the identical name of the sailor and chauffer being a bizarre coincidence.

Another strange event connected to Captain Colvocoresses occurred. Just a little over four summers following the captain's death, during August 1876, Colvos's old insurance agent, Alfred Smith, pushed back from his desk, grabbed his tackle box and headed north for a needed vacation. In Sharon, Massachusetts, something peculiarly tragic happened to the zealous adjuster whose investigation had pointed to Colvos's death as a suicide. Fishing on a small pond with his father, Smith's boat capsized. Knowing the pond wasn't very deep, the elder man swam to shore, thinking his son could care for himself. Instead, the agent became entangled in the lines and drowned. Investigators felt that Smith, who couldn't swim, should have at least been able to cling to the craft. But inexplicably, when Smith's body was recovered, his hands appeared as if they'd been tied with fishing wire. Police noted the insurance man was completely smeared with mud—as if he'd been wrestling on the bottom of the pond.

One can only imagine silent nods in smoky harbor-side saloons and retired sailors' homes, up and down the Connecticut coast, when the news of that fishing accident came through their doors. It was as if the agent who tried to drag down the reputation of an old sailor was himself caught by long, mossy fingers and pulled into that cold New England pond.

The Strange Notebook of Dr. George Porter, Reanimator

1880, 1888

A quest amid black and forbidden realms of the unknown, in which he hoped to uncover the secret of life and restore to perpetual animation the graveyard's cold clay. Such a quest demands strange materials, among them fresh human bodies.
—H.P. Lovecraft, "Herbert West—Reanimator," 1922

Dr. George Porter, an army surgeon, has been trying to bring the body of an executed murderer to life in Bridgeport, Conn.
—New York Tribune, *June 11, 1880*

Make no mistake—Dr. George Loring Porter is a member of that rare breed of American adventurer-hero. Yet it is the longtime Bridgeport resident's unmistakable and historic attachment to death that brings this surgeon's tale to life. A life that harbored one of the nineteenth century's greatest secrets; a secret that reached the highest office in the land and would, in the surgeon's own words, "not be revealed until long after" his own demise. Yet even more fantastical are Dr. Porter's alchemic writings concerning attempts to raise the dead.

George Porter was as rugged and deep-rooted a New Englander as the granite from his home state, New Hampshire. Born in 1838, his ancestors arrived in Massachusetts two hundred years earlier during the witch-fearing seventeenth century. Porter attended schools in Maine and New Hampshire and later, in 1859, graduated from Brown University while secessionist war clouds gathered over our soon-to-be-divided nation. In May 1862, less than a month after completing his medical degree at Jefferson College in Philadelphia, he joined the Union army. Destiny cradled a unique place for Porter. Stationed in the Shenandoah Valley, the doctor volunteered to remain behind tending to the sick and wounded during the North's retreat. After Porter was captured by Virginia cavalry, Stonewall Jackson recognized his value and requested the friend-prisoner to care for both Union and Confederate injured. The twenty-four-year-old humanitarian left an impact; fifty-three years later, parishioners of the Presbyterian Church in Strasburg, site of the field hospital, invited their old "enemy" back for a hero's welcome.

When Union forces again swept into the Shenandoah, Porter returned to his unit and was promoted to assistant surgeon with the rank of first lieutenant. He often performed surgery under fire during the Battles of Fredericksburg, Gettysburg, Brandy Station, Second Bull Run and Boonsboro, where he received a wound to his left arm. On April 29, 1864, the first lieutenant was ordered to report for duty in Washington, D.C., but the fog of war waylaid the correspondence, compelling Porter to take part in the terrifying Battle of the Wilderness. Due to an order lost, an untold number of lives were saved by the brave New Englander. After the battle, Porter took charge of the wounded on his way north to the capital.

Dr. George Loring Porter, of Bridgeport, was involved with the science of galvanism and attempts to raise the dead. *Courtesy of the Bridgeport Public Library, Bridgeport History Center.*

Lieutenant Porter became the medical officer at the Washington Arsenal during the year leading up to Appomattox, when Lee surrendered to Grant, ending the Civil War. Events were taking form in the capital that would soon thrust the surgeon into one of the greatest government conspiracies of all time.

On April 14, 1865, the nation was grievously shocked when Abraham Lincoln was assassinated at Ford's Theatre by actor John Wilkes Booth. The goal of the assassin and his co-conspirators was to plunge the federal government into chaos. The strategy quickly unraveled when the man assigned to kill Vice President Johnson lost his nerve and the assault on

General John F. Hartranft and his staff were responsible for securing the Lincoln assassination conspirators at the Washington Arsenal, April–July 1865. Assistant Surgeon George L. Porter, who oversaw the prisoners' medical well-being, recommended the removal of torturous canvas hoods; he is standing on the far right. *Courtesy of the Library of Congress, LC-DIG-cwpb-04199.*

Secretary of State Seward failed. Booth and fellow conspirator David Herold were pursued into Northern Virginia and cornered on the Garrett Farm, where Booth was shot dead and Herold was taken into custody.

The assassin's body was transported to Washington, where an autopsy was performed aboard the monitor *Montauk*. Afterward, two officers were seen rowing a small boat down the Anacostia River where, under the cloak of dark, they dumped a wrapped corpse into a murky swamp reserved for the army's dead mules. Neither disgust nor fear of disease stopped the curious from wading through the morass, feeling their way among animal bones and rotting flesh in an unsuccessful search for the despised Booth. In reality, sliding the shrouded figure into the river was a ruse carefully orchestrated by Secretary of War Edwin Stanton. What actually transpired with Booth's remains during the wee hours of April 28, 1865, remained a secret that Dr. Porter vowed would not be revealed until after his own death.

At midnight on the twenty-eighth, the arsenal's storekeeper, four enlisted men and Lieutenant Porter, the only commissioned officer present, escorted Booth's authentic earthly remains from a boathouse on the river's banks through the arsenal grounds and into the old army penitentiary. The storekeeper unlocked the massive door to a crate-filled storeroom. Sewn

President Abraham Lincoln's assassin, John Wilkes Booth. The secrecy assigned to the actor's burial spawned decades of popular myth that he had survived the raid on his hideout at Garrett's Farm in Northern Virginia. *Courtesy of the Library of Congress, LC-DIG-ppmsca-19233.*

inside a gunnysack and then bound in an army blanket, Booth's body was placed in a shallow hole in the enclosure's southwest corner and covered. Secretary Stanton ultimately came to hold the lone key to this lurid chamber. Clandestine movements attached with these remains stirred popular folk belief that John Wilkes Booth had actually escaped. Four years later, Edwin Booth, the assassin's brother, successfully petitioned President Johnson to allow the decomposed body to be reinterred in the family's Maryland plot. Edwin refused to gaze upon the corpse (which, oddly enough, he received in an alley next to Ford's Theatre), once again fanning rumors that the assassin had survived and fled to parts unknown. For decades, from Cos Cob, Connecticut, to Granbury, Texas, old gray-mustached men with a strangely familiar flair for quoting Shakespeare claimed that they were John Wilkes Booth. The mystery surrounding the exact location of the murderer's burial spot reinforced these Booth imposters' act for forty-plus years.

In 1865, during the conspirators' trial, Dr. Porter was placed in charge of the prisoners' medical care. There were upward of forty suspects being held in the old penitentiary. Porter alone was allowed to speak with the incarcerated without being accompanied by soldiers. Ever the humanitarian, the surgeon requested that the torturous canvas head wraps, encasing all but the mouth and small area of the nose, be removed from these individuals. He also insisted that books and exercise be allowed. An alienist agreed with Porter's opinion that the sensory-deprivation hoods could cause insanity. The canvas devices were eliminated from the majority of suspects; however, for those prisoners who were part of Booth's inner circle, Secretary Stanton had the coverings replaced with tighter-fitting hoods lined with thick cotton, an even more torturous devise in the steamy Washington summer. At the trial's conclusion, Mrs. Mary Surratt, Lewis Powell (aka Paine), David Herold and George Atzerodt were found guilty and led to the gallows. When the trapdoors snapped open, Dr. Porter and two other physicians officially pronounced the four conspirators dead; it was the first instance of a woman being hanged in the United States. (Interestingly, Dr. Porter would later be present during the autopsy of another presidential assassin, Charles Guiteau, the deranged man who killed President James Garfield in 1882.)

Following the execution of the Lincoln assassins, Porter was promoted to captain and ordered to deliver the remaining conspirators—Samuel Arnold, Michael O'Laughlin and Edward Spangler, along with Dr. Samuel Mudd (who aided Booth and mended his leg after fleeing Ford's Theatre)—to the island prison on Dry Tortugas.

The execution of Booth's co-conspirators, July 7, 1865. *Left to right*: Mrs. Mary Surratt, Lewis Powell, David Herold and George Atzerodt. Lieutenant Porter was among the medical staff confirming that the death sentence was carried out. Afterward, Porter escorted four other conspirators to the island prison on Dry Tortugas. *Courtesy of the Library of Congress, LC-DIG-cwpb-04230.*

Up until this time, Porter's family had resided in Rhode Island, but after escorting these prisoners to the remote fortress seventy miles off Key West, the doctor began to consider relocating to Bridgeport. Porter was familiar with the Park City, as there are references in his journal about family and acquaintances living here. On the return trip north from Florida, the side-wheeler USS *Florida* docked in New York, and the surgeon took a train to Bridgeport, where he enjoyed a visit with an aunt. On the evening of August 1, 1865, Porter meandered along Bridgeport's avenues with his dear friend Dr. Robert Hubbard during a long carriage ride. In his diary, Porter expressively notes, "[Hubbard] advised me very sensibly to select first of all a pleasant place to live in, and a good place to bring up a family; [my medical] practice would come in time." A month later, Porter's daughter, little Bessie, died in Providence. Hubbard's sound advice, combined with the sad memories lingering in the Porters' Rhode Island home, prompted the doctor to move his family to Bridgeport.

Plans to relocate to the Nutmeg State were delayed, however. Now drawing a major's pay, Porter was ordered in 1867 to quit his post in Washington and report to Camp Cook, Montana, hostile Indian territory. Here he cared for soldiers wounded by Indian arrows as well as members of local tribes, built an army hospital and delivered babies. Venturing outside the fort to assist a Native American deathly ill with pneumonia, Porter was presented with a papoose as payment for saving the woman. The doctor relished his time in the wilderness and the opportunity to travel in Lewis and Clark's footsteps. A year later, upon resigning his commission, he continued westward to the Pacific, sometimes on horseback and other days alone on foot, to complete the famous explorers' route. Porter then sailed from the West Coast southward, where he crossed the jungle isthmus at Panama. From here, the doctor returned to Bridgeport, where he established life as a civilian. Little did the retired soldier realize that his old attachment to death would have a bizarre new beginning.

George L. Porter was embraced as one of the Park City's leading lights. In addition to his medical practice, the surgeon was an incorporator of Bridgeport Hospital and served on its executive committee. He was president of the Fairfield Medical Association and the Connecticut Medical Society, and from 1876 to 1877, Porter was president of the Bridgeport Medical Association. His prowess as an orator was regularly called upon. The doctor addressed medical societies, veterans' organizations and social clubs across the state. He was also one of the official speakers who helped dedicate the Barnum Institute of Science and History, which later became the Barnum Museum, and he delivered the opening address for Bridgeport Hospital's surgical building.

Death, however, was not through with Dr. Porter. Like his earlier connection with the Lincoln conspirators, his next strange brush with the beyond took place during another hanging. Thirty-six-year-old Sherman, Connecticut resident Edwin Hoyt's mind was scrambled from longtime abuse of apple jack when, on June 23, 1878, he jabbed a butcher knife into his father's jugular. The old man had been a stern and abusive parent, a trait Edwin sadly inherited and employed throughout his own days, from bullying schoolmates to beating his wife. Distraught by difficulties he'd faced supporting his family, combined with the perception of a sibling conspiracy aimed at separating him from his inheritance, Edwin had become increasingly hostile. An argument erupted when he demanded property from his father. Edwin returned to his own home, donned a clean set of clothes, sharpened a knife and told his wife "he was going to kill the old man." Even after being tackled to the ground, his hands and clothes splashed with his father's blood, Edwin steadfastly claimed he could not remember attacking his dad. He blamed his dementia on alcohol and mind fevers he had begun suffering during military service nearly two decades earlier. Hoyt's attorneys argued insanity, but two trials and a number of well-intentioned legal maneuvers still ultimately resulted in the death penalty. The date set for execution was May 13, 1880. The governor declined to intervene.

During the legal proceedings, Edwin remained incarcerated for over a year in Bridgeport's North Avenue jail. The night before his sentence was to be carried out, he listened to one of the guards exclaim how particularly beautiful the apple blossoms were that season. Edwin interrupted the jailer, sharing how he'd love to have just three weeks to visit the apple orchards. He promised to return, and anyone who ever knew Edwin admitted that he never did utter a lie. Edwin Hoyt's last night on earth was spent conversing with his jailers. Asked if Edwin cared to make a final statement from the gallows, the prisoner said he'd have nothing to say that wasn't expressed in the letters he'd pen during the final hours he faced. Questioned about an autopsy being performed, Hoyt agreed, as long as it was done by a familiar doctor and his body wasn't sent to some medical college; he was especially anxious for physicians to find out what illness caused a lifetime of mental anguish.

The scaffold was erected in New Haven and transported to Bridgeport with ironic timing. The wooden platform and its hanging apparatus were delivered by truck directly behind the parade ballyhooing the circus coming to town. Hoyt asked a guard if he'd be visiting the circus. When the turnkey said he wouldn't be attending, the condemned man sarcastically commented that his hanging offered "a bigger circus tomorrow" and "they'd both be going."

The next morning, Hoyt was led out through the jail window and down a temporary staircase built to avoid the five hundred people who'd assembled to witness his hanging. In accordance with the law, the execution was to be private, so the gallows rested within an enclosure that had been erected earlier in the week on the west side of the jail. Only those with tickets to the execution were allowed inside the wooden stockade. Folks lacking the sheriff's passes were offering up to ten dollars to anyone willing to part with the gruesome ducat. The *Bridgeport Leader* recorded that the pen was filled with tobacco smoke, jesting and profanity.

Abruptly, the crowd quieted. Sheriff Aaron Sanford emerged from the window, dressed in black and wearing a high silk hat. Behind him two deputies appeared, followed by Edwin, his head bent. Reverend Eaton W. Maxcy walked beside the prisoner; the Episcopal minister rested an arm on the condemned man, who'd just been baptized hours before. Behind them, two more deputies marched. Then came four physicians: Drs. Porter, Robert Lauder, Edwin DeWitt Nooney and James Marshall. The wish Hoyt had expressed the previous night came to fruition at that moment. Crossing the narrow grounds and ascending the steps leading to the noose, Edwin glanced upon a blossoming apple tree off to the side of the gallows.

The prisoner stretched a purple finger out from his bound fists to shake hands and thank his jailer, the reverend and his guards. Prayers and verdict were read aloud while Edwin peacefully sat in a chair that was placed in the platform's center. The noose and black hood were fitted. After Edwin was helped to his feet by the guards, Sheriff Sanford stepped forward, grabbed Edwin's fingers and said, "Goodbye, poor fellow." A muffled "Goodbye" came from within the hood. At 11:39 a.m., the wooden trap opened, and Hoyt fell into eternity.

Hanging from the end of the manila rope, Dr. Lauder pressed a wrist; Dr. Porter counted the beats and duly recorded them in his notebook. At noon, the two doctors, one after the other, placed an ear to the swaying man's chest. No heartbeat was detected. More time was allowed to fulfill the state's decree that Edwin Hoyt should "hang by the neck until dead." A fellow prisoner who'd been spared the death penalty had requested to watch the macabre proceedings from a barred widow. He cupped a watch in his hands, timing Edwin's final moments. Tears streamed down his face. It was now 12:15 p.m. Hoyt had remained dangling for thirty-five minutes.

Suddenly, the scene was all a rush. Removed from the gallows, Hoyt's lifeless body was placed on a coffin lid and raced to the jail's second-floor hospital facility. Those still milling out from the wooden enclosure's doorway turned back to stare at the odd excitement. Upstairs, the medical room and special equipment had been properly prepared to Dr. Porter's wishes. The space filled with twenty physicians, in addition to guards, the ministers Maxcy and Charles E. Harris and a number of local wealthy merchants. A plan had been set in motion to see whether Edwin Hoyt could be brought back to life through the use of "galvanism." Someone in the throng asked, should the experiment prove successful, would Edwin have to be hanged again? No one offered a reply.

The scientific study of galvanism dated back to the 1780s, when Italian physician Luigi Galvani demonstrated that electricity made dead frogs twitch. Following a decade of study, he shocked the medical world with his

The gruesome effects of galvanism as applied to the decapitated heads of executed French criminals during the 1860s. Frank Leslie's Illustrated Newspaper, *December 29, 1866; Michael J. Bielawa Collection.*

1791 publication, "Commentary on the Effects of Electricity on Muscular Motion." The Bolognese doctor concluded that the source of all life is derived from a form of innate "animal electricity," soon popularly labeled "galvanism." After Galvani's death, his nephew, Professor Giovanni Aldini, carried the banner of galvanism, switching experiments from cold-blooded frogs to warm-blooded subjects, such as oxen, dogs and human corpses. In early 1803, Aldini was invited to London, where he applied galvanism to an executed criminal. The muscular movements elicited from the deceased man astounded the Royal College of Surgeons; it was eagerly anticipated that such a procedure would work to resuscitate drowning victims.

Over the next few decades, galvanistic investigations spread far afield, tantalizing Europe and the United States. Utilizing this chilling new concept, Mary Shelley coaxed her waking nightmare, Frankenstein, to life. Due to its being hawked by quacks as a cure-all, antebellum America became very familiar with its pseudo-applications. One 1846 *Hartford Daily Courant* advertisement casually announced a "safe and novel application of the mysterious power of Galvanism," guaranteeing "entire success in all cases of" rheumatism, gout, toothache, bronchitis, vertigo, nervous or sick headache, indigestion, paralysis, palsy, epilepsy, fits, cramps and general debility.

Moments after being cut free of his noose, on the afternoon of May 13, 1880, Edwin Hoyt's corpse lay before a gathering of Bridgeport notables. The first order of business was to determine whether Hoyt had died because

Public awareness of galvanism was so widespread in America during the first half of the nineteenth century that the science was even lampooned in this 1836 political cartoon. *Courtesy of the Library of Congress, LC-USZ62-11916.*

of suffocation or a broken neck, as the latter would derail the experiment. The doctors in the room pronounced that the spine was intact, merely dislocated, and that the procedure should move ahead. An incision was made above the clavicle, and wires from "a single cell Kidder electro-galvanic battery, capable of giving a very powerful current," were then applied to the phrenic nerve and diaphragm. Respiration was simulated. The doctors remarked how Hoyt seemed to be simply sleeping. The wetted electrodes were now attached to the muscles of the forearms, upper arms and shoulders, causing the corpse's arms to thrash about and point accusingly at the merchants and holy men assembled. More startling were the facial expressions created by the galvanic charge; the doctors gasped when Edwin opened his eyes and stared. Dr. Porter noted in his official paper, read before the Bridgeport Medical Society at Dr. Lauder's home, "The face produced expressions of joy and surprise, and anger and fright." The executed man frighteningly rolled his eyeballs at the assemblage, pausing to glare, and then "savagely frowned." For an hour and a half, the medical staff inflicted morbid grimaces upon the dead man. However, hopes to restart the heart failed. An unnamed physician, most likely Porter, remarked, "Could we have made the heart move we would have had some hope of being able to resuscitate the man…We were at the very portals of the mystery of life and death." The unnamed doctor mused, "We had induced natural respiration. If we could have made the heart beat…it would have been actually raising the dead to life." Why hadn't the experiment brought Edwin back to the world of the living? Despondently, the physicians noted they had misdiagnosed Hoyt's spinal injury; his back had indeed been broken during the fall through the trapdoor. Dr. Porter's report concludes, "Restoration to life of the supposed dead by stimulation… may be [created by] an example of mechanical revival." Viewing the results of the day's experiments, the thought must certainly have crossed more than one doctor's mind that the only thing needed to further explore galvanism was a fresh, untainted body. It turned out to be an eight-year wait.

In a long-simmering fit of rage, Philip Palladino (some write Palladoni) killed his brother Francisco over a forty-dollar loan. Fran was too slow in repaying the money he had borrowed to emigrate from Italy. On June 22, 1887, Philip sought comeuppance. Hiding near Pierce's Quarry in Fairfield, where the brothers worked, he shot his sibling dead. Palladino was arrested, brought to trial and hanged on October 5, 1888. Drs. Lauder and Porter were again part of the medical team. In a morbid twist of fate, the scaffold erected was the same one that had claimed Edwin Hoyt; it stood just a few feet from the exact spot it had back in 1880, in the jail's west yard. Palladino firmly trod up the platform's stairs, but glancing up at the noose, he became faint and faltered. When the trap opened a few moments later, the black hood flew off Palladino, and the cap needed to be replaced over the head of the swinging body (the hood was later publicly exhibited at the police station). After that, all proceeded as expected, except a fracas erupted when Palladino's body was lowered into the plain pine coffin waiting beneath the gallows. Jailhouse physician Robert Lauder placed a hand on the dead man's neck to ascertain if it was broken, and "a violent scene" ensued. Palladino's priest, Father Leo, burst forward, waving his arms excitedly, and demanded no one touch the body. The priest was intent on protecting the deceased from being experimented upon.

Then the wild stories began. Rumors circulating in New York and New Haven indicated that Palladino was miraculously still among the living. At first there was a belief that the condemned man had been buried alive. That tale quickly gave way to the belief that Palladino and Father Leo, among others in the gallows and burial crew, were members of an ancient Italian secret society. The clandestine order came to the condemned fellow's rescue by suiting him with a special brace beneath his clothes. When Palladino

Philip Palladino murdered his brother over an unpaid debt and was executed in Bridgeport on October 5, 1888. Strange events began happening immediately after his hanging. *Courtesy of the Connecticut State Library.*

feigned falling sideways on the gallows, the guard or priest helping the prisoner to his feet slipped a steel hook into a hidden leather collar. This device negated the deadly effects of the noose. Because Palladino was faking his death, it was argued, Father Leo purposely caused the jail yard commotion when he saw the body about to be examined.

Other tales were told as well, all based on plans to reanimate the dead man. Doctors realized, unlike the Hoyt experiment eight years earlier, that Palladino's neck was not broken. Fears were raised that unscrupulous physicians, or a team of resurrection men under their employ, would disinter the body and deliver it for galvanic experiments. An unnamed Bridgeport doctor shared his thoughts on the matter: "Palladino was a beautiful subject for an electrical experiment. He was of robust body, and his neck not being broken, there was excellent material for the galvanic battery to work upon. Had it chanced by a bare possibility that our treatment brought him back to life, I presume he would have gone free, as the law had visited upon him the prescribed penalty." A sentinel was positioned at the grave site within St. Augustine cemetery to prevent any grave desecration. Father Leo and the Italian community were successful; the morning after the hanging, the burial mound remained undisturbed.

Over the ensuing days, Bridgeport newspaper editors pleaded with their New York and New Haven counterparts to stop the parade of fantastical assertions about Palladino being alive and to "let the dead rest." But the supernatural clamor also had other unwelcome results. Within a week of the execution, guards in the west yard of the jailhouse started to complain that they felt as though someone, unseen, was watching them.

The Palladino incident was the last reported attempt at reanimating the dead in the city of Bridgeport. Dr. Porter's strange writings on the subject are a matter of public record, having been reprinted in Connecticut and New York newspapers. Still, George Porter's perplexing brushes with death were not complete. As the nineteenth century approached its conclusion, reminiscences and histories of the Civil War abounded. There were many instances when authors noted that Dr. Porter had died. It was with a bit of humor that the surgeon felt compelled to address his own demise. In a 1909 issue of the *New York Times*, his letter to the editor vowed, in the words of Mark Twain, that rumors of his "death are generally greatly exaggerated." Death, however, would eventually catch up with Porter. The doctor passed from this life quite peacefully while vacationing in Florida on February 24, 1919. His body was brought back to Bridgeport and the New England he loved. There is no record of any attempt to reanimate the body. Galvanism wasn't necessary to resurrect the surgeon; the adventures experienced by Dr. George Loring Porter generated electricity enough to keep his memory alive for several lifetimes.

Swamp Road Slaughterhouse

1882

Folks along the Connecticut shore have always been a superstitious lot. The two burly Bridgeporters peering uneasily into the winter's gloom shrouding Swamp Road were no exception. It was late January 1883, and this was the night the pair had chosen to settle a macabre wager. Lingering tales of homes haunted by murder victims had led these Bridgeport men to challenge each other over remaining an entire night locked in Phoebe Brush's abandoned cottage. It was less than a month since the pretty, thirty-five-year-old mulatto had met her tragic end at the hands of an axe-wielding fiend. A madman who, incidentally, was still on the loose. Several grisly blows had been administered to her face and scalp, but the first mighty stroke, directly behind Phoebe's left ear, did the job. It nearly severed her head from her shoulders. The gambling men discussed the ghostly challenge awaiting them as they approached the gruesome crime site. Seeing the bloodstained plank floors, they began to wrestle over the notion of whether it was worth an eight-dollar bet to shiver alone in this lurid house on such a cold night.

Phoebe Brush had lived alone. She hadn't seen her absent husband, William, for roughly four years. Back about 1875, after only six weeks of marriage, Mr. Brush was sentenced to two years in state prison for robbery. Following his jail time, William attempted to get back with Phoebe, but he'd been physically abusive, and Phoebe would hear nothing of reconciliation. For a while, Phoebe's sister, Delia, and toddler niece stayed at the Swamp Road home. The lonely shack in neighboring Stratford, consisting of two rooms and an attic, was situated in a wooded area not

Beautiful Phoebe Brush lived alone in an old slaughterhouse and was murdered with an axe. Curious Bridgeport ghost hunters visited the spot to settle a bet. This photograph was recovered by detectives investigating the case in 1883. *Courtesy of Historical & Special Collections, Harvard Law School Library.*

far from the marshes leading out to the lighthouse. It was an ideal spot for the structure's original purpose—a slaughterhouse. It certainly was a forlorn location, but the attractive woman did have her visitors. For a year now, a gentleman caller, Henry Freeman of Meriden, Connecticut, had been taking the train down to the shore in order to be with Phoebe. He promised Phoebe that he would soon divorce his present wife and marry the comely Stratford woman.

On Saturday, December 30, 1882, Mrs. Brush sat in her chair busying herself knitting a mitten. It would be her final earthly chore. She was found the next day, Sunday, by her Baptist brethren when they ventured to the cottage requesting Phoebe to take part in services. "How odd," the churchmen thought as they were approaching the shack, "to have a lantern burning on so bright a day." They knocked on the front door and entered when no one responded. The visitors were shocked to discover Phoebe lying in a pool of blood. A shawl partially covered her where she lay in the kitchen, her head rested across the doorsill entering the living room. The chair where she had sat was overturned. Phoebe's face lay on its right cheek, exposing the brutal gash behind the left ear, cut so deep it severed her spinal chord. The clump of yarn she was occupied with was still twined around her finger; a gold ring was missing from her hand. Near Phoebe's feet, an axe matted with blood and hair leaned against the wall.

SUSPECTS ABOUND

Stratford constable Abijah McEwen and Justice Eugene Morehouse were summoned. Word spread quickly through the quiet village, and the officials were joined on their march to the cottage by a growing throng of townsfolk. The men examined the deceased, interviewed the Baptist visitors and searched the house. A letter written in Phoebe's hand and addressed to "Henry P. Freeman, Meriden, Conn.," was found on a table next to the kerosene lamp. The envelope had been carefully cut open along one end with scissors. Inside were an intimate letter and a tintype featuring the pretty young victim. A trunk revealed another thirty or so love letters from Freeman, the substance of which indicated that he often visited. Freeman's most recent note, dated December 21, expressed his plans to visit her on Saturday, December 30. Police now had some concrete leads; Freeman needed to be questioned, as well as Mr. Brush. Had the estranged husband returned for the holiday only to explode into a jealous rage when he uncovered these letters? Stratford lacked a regular police force, so professional assistance was sought from Bridgeport, as well as from Pinkerton agents.

The crime solvers determined that the culprit obviously was no stranger to Phoebe Brush; otherwise, the victim would not have been calmly knitting at the time of the attack. Being that the lantern was left burning and most of the fuel spent, it was determined that the murder had been accomplished the previous evening or night. Another suspect in the case was Phoebe's brother, John "Six-Fingered Jack" Gilbert, who was rumored to have been on bad terms with his sibling. Six-Fingered Jack was immediately questioned, but his alibi and whereabouts were confirmed, removing him from suspicion. There were other suspects as well. By a strange coincidence, the conductor on the milk train from New Haven remembered an African American man boarding the cars in New Haven with a ticket for Bridgeport, but he got off in Stratford and headed toward the center of town. A stranger was reported seen in the vicinity of Phoebe's house on Saturday, "a light skinned, short fellow in a stiff hat." The next day, a fellow of the same description came into the yard of neighbor Ruth Whitfield asking for cigars.

WHAT'S LOVE GOT TO DO WITH IT?

Authorities felt all those love letters announced that the murder may have been a crime of passion. Phoebe's younger and, as locals noted, "prettier" sister, Delia Gilbert, was rumored to be involved with Henry Freeman as well. Delia, who was pregnant, admitted she had gone down to the Stratford depot the night of the murder to greet the Meriden man, but he never arrived. Any amorous relationship between Freeman and Delia would soon be thrown into serious doubt. It turned out that Henry Freeman was accountable during Saturday; he never left his central Connecticut city the night in question.

BOSTON AND DELIA

When Phoebe's body was first discovered, Bridgeport Officer George Arnold and Detective Taylor went to Delia Gilbert's north Stratford home to inquire about the murdered woman's acquaintances. When the officers knocked on the door, a lantern inside the house was quickly extinguished. A number of minutes passed before Delia answered their pounding, and she initially refused to admit the police. When the authorities finally gained entrance and explained the reason for their visit, Delia "expressed no surprise or regret" and was anxious that they leave. Newspapers reported that she acted "as if she were secreting something or someone."

On New Year's Day, Officer Arnold returned to Delia's home, where she ran down a checklist of her Saturday activities. She paid a long overdue coal bill, stopped by the train depot anticipating her sister to be there, went grocery shopping and then went back home. Gilbert was visibly nervous while her closet was searched and her clothing and a pair of overshoes were inspected. The alpaca sacque she wore that fateful Saturday revealed several spots resembling faded blood; Delia admitted that she had washed the garments Sunday night, the day after the murder. When the policeman removed this evidence from her house, she exclaimed, "Well, that won't tell any tales!"

It was rumored that on the morning after the police first knocked on Delia's door, a man was seen leaving her home. Most likely that person was Boston White. "Boss" was the nineteen-year-old son of Civil War hero Boston B. White; the young man's father had enlisted in the famous Connecticut 29th Colored Regiment and was among the first U.S. troops to enter the Confederate capital after its fall in 1865. Boston Jr. admitted before the inquiry that he had visited Delia on the Friday before Phoebe's murder and had been in Delia's home Sunday night. Yes, he knew Phoebe; he had first met her a year before through Delia, but he insisted that he'd last seen the victim two weeks prior to her death at church. Boss enjoyed impressing the yokels with a "bad man" image, womanizing, boozing and with his fisticuffs. His statements shocked folks when it became known that Delia was carrying Boston White's baby and that Boston also bragged about an incestuous relationship with his aunt.

Delia was unavailable for questioning due to a difficult pregnancy. She gave birth to Boss's son on January 5, after which Officer Arnold intensified his inquiries. When Delia was healthy enough to talk, she underwent a three-hour interview on January 12. Arnold's daily questioning was agitating. On Monday, January 15, when the officer rose to leave, Delia grasped his arm and made a strange plea: "Oh, if I could only trust you!" Arnold said that she could trust him, and the woman promised to "tell the whole story," but only after consulting with her attorney. The next day, she had a change of heart. Delia's intense examination over the course of four days found the pretty suspect contradicting her previous statements, and eventually she refused to answer any more questions.

As Boss White's bizarre connection with the crime began to raise eyebrows, William Brush was finally located by Pinkerton agents. Phoebe's husband was arrested at his Thirty-eighth Street residence in New York City and brought to Bridgeport for questioning. Mr. Brush happily complied, stating that he had not seen his former wife for some time; divorce proceedings were being finalized, and he had no knowledge whatsoever of Phoebe's death, having only found out about the sad event with his arrest.

AN ANONYMOUS LETTER

Just after the murder became public, Bridgeport police chief William E. Marsh received an anonymous letter implicating East Bridgeport resident Edward "Irish" McGuirk in the crime. McGuirk was an unsavory character who had just returned to town after being implicated with an earlier stabbing. Local papers appealed to the letter's mysterious author to come forward and hinted at a reward. The unsigned letter painted a disturbing tale of McGuirk being seen on Sunday, December 31, at about two o'clock in the morning running along the Stratford railroad tracks. When hailed, McGuirk shouted that he had just had a fight with a "fellow" and "downed him." McGuirk was called in for questioning on January 8. He explained that he'd known Phoebe for five or six years and often stopped at her place for a drink of water. During the week prior to the murder, he was hunting in the marsh near Phoebe's shack when his dogs charged into her yard, chasing the woman's cat. Angered, Phoebe came out of the house with an axe, threatening to kill McGuirk if he ever set foot on her property again.

Seven days after the police interrogation, Irish McGuirk was arrested and placed in solitary confinement in the Bridgeport police station. On Thursday, January 16, after a six-day incarceration, a beaming William Brush was allowed to return to New York City. Meanwhile, in solitary confinement, Irish McGuirk was repeatedly cross-examined and finally allowed to write to his mother. Unknown to McGuirk, this liberty was just a ploy to acquire a writing sample. It matched the anonymous note's hand, and McGuirk confessed to staging the episode for notoriety's sake. McGuirk, the vile specimen he was, reveled in his successful strategy of thwarting the police and making fools of the Pinkertons.

CIRCUMSTANTIAL EVIDENCE BUILDS

The day after McGuirk's release, on January 24, Delia Gilbert was taken into custody with a warrant signed by the grand jury. Officers walked into a freezing home; Delia lay in bed, her newborn on one side of her and her toddler on the other. The children escorted their mother into the cell at the Bridgeport police station. Delia's mother tried to visit her at the station, but she got no farther than the Bridgeport train depot, where emotions overcame the woman. Officer Arnold pacified her shrieking hysterics and placed her back on a Stratford-bound train. Six-Finger Jack, Delia's brother, came to police headquarters too, threatening officers, but he was sent on his way.

Three days later, Delia and her two children were removed from their cell and transported by horse carriage to Stratford Town Hall. A huge crowd was on hand. Represented by attorney E.F. Hall, Delia loudly pronounced "not guilty." During the hearing, Officer Arnold testified about his interrogating Delia—how agitated and peculiar the suspect had acted when questioned, and how she stalled to admit officers into her house on the Sunday evening after the murder. Arnold also explained that during one visit, Phoebe's sister blurted out "that a woman did the deed."

During the hearing, undertaker William H. Curtis stated that the shawl found on the deceased was not placed there afterward to cover the victim but was worn by Phoebe and fell across her body as she slumped to the floor. Witnesses did place Delia in lower Stratford that Saturday night. Emmett Beardsley, who knew both sisters, said he saw either Delia or Phoebe on Lundy's Lane not far from the crime site. Joseph Dufour, a harness maker, testified that Delia was at the Stratford train depot just after the 7:09 p.m. train had left. She was heading east, in the direction away from Phoebe's house. The witness explained that Delia "looked very strange," and Dufour asked "what she was afraid of." Delia said nothing "but stopped and seemed very much excited." Probable cause was found, and Delia remained behind bars without bail at Bridgeport's North Avenue Jail while the state prepared for trial.

A HAUNTING CRIME

Evidence proved lacking. Delia explained that the bloodstains on the dress she wore the night of the killing were from liver that had leaked through its wrapper days before the murder. The butcher corroborated Delia's visit to the shop. Dr. Moses C. White, a blood expert in New Haven, could not conclusively provide answers. The clothing had been thoroughly washed the day after the crime. The bloodstain on the sole of Delia's overshoes was tainted with dirt and other material. The state's ace in the hole, a bloodstain and hand mark on a trunk owned by Phoebe, revealed itself to be red paint. Delia Gilbert was released from jail on May 12, 1883. Eventually, she vanished from town. The *Bridgeport Evening Farmer* observed, "It now looks as if the killing of Phoebe Brush would remain one of the unsolved mysteries of the times."

Boston White was implicated in yet another Stratford murder that same year, but concrete evidence was again sorely lacking. Boss did wind up in a cell for a short stint during December 1883 for assault. The following summer, he abducted a married New Milford woman he'd been involved with, yet he beat prosecution again. If Boston had any connection with the Brush murder, his guilty conscience might have caught up with him. On New Year's Day 1942, almost fifty-nine years to the moment that Phoebe Brush's mutilated body was discovered, Boss died. George Arnold went on to become chief of police in Bridgeport. He'd be forever haunted by the unresolved crime. As late as 1906, he lamented how Bridgeport residents still taunted him about Phoebe Brush.

As for the two gambling friends peering into Phoebe's dark shack, the fellow who had agreed to remain locked all night alone in Mrs. Brush's eerie cottage experienced a change of heart. It was much too cold to spend a winter's night in an abandoned house. Lacking a fire, his friend suggested that the curious ghost hunter curl up in Phoebe's bed there in the corner. On that shuddering thought, the two men turned back down Swamp Road, heading home for Bridgeport, the wiser fellow eight dollars poorer.

No One Gets Out of Here Alive

1886–1905

The Suicide Club, why, what the devil is that?
—*Robert Louis Stevenson,* The Suicide Club, *1878*

Something sinister inhabited the bustling neighborhood near Bridgeport's brick Victorian railway station. This was during the late 1800s, back before the rails were elevated, when the New York, New Haven & Hartford Railroad depot greeted passengers on street level at the foot of Fairfield Avenue. Jostled on steel Pullmans from across America, cigar-wielding business executives and derby-adorned salesmen dodged horse-drawn wagons of all description to cross Water Street for a room in the Atlantic Hotel. Visitors with a little time on their hands longing for Old World atmosphere need only manage a short walk from the tracks. The adjacent part of downtown, around Bank Street, housed an enclave of German and Swiss immigrants. The quarter was known for its jovial tavern keepers as much as its festive Saturday night beef dinners and delicious, ever-flowing beer. But also set back among these alleys were certain abodes festering with a tangible melancholy. Subterfuge concerning the following strange events precludes definitive answers, but as word spread, eventually the whole world would come to regard these Bridgeport doorways as portals to madness.

John Kienzy was the proprietor of the saloon where the Suicide Club came to life. *Courtesy of the Connecticut State Library.*

Bridgeport's world-renowned showman and fervent temperance champion, P.T. Barnum, lamented that his own city tolerated nearly three hundred drinking establishments; mathematically, that equated to one saloon for every fifteen Park City men. One of the most popular spots was John Kienzy's. His pub was situated on Main Street near Congress Avenue. The Swiss fellow was popular throughout town, especially within Bridgeport's German-speaking community. Sporting a fashionable handlebar mustache and slinging steins of beer, the bartender often entertained patrons with songs from the old country. John was a member of the Concordia Singing Society, as well as an excellent marksman. He was proud of the competitive awards he won with a local rifle team.

His tavern was a magnet to German and Swiss expatriates, who enjoyed evenings deep in philosophical discussion. Among them were sign painter William Meckel, musician and fellow saloon owner Victor Heisterhagen and hotel proprietor Wendell Baum. These gentlemen had gathered at Kienzy's establishment one particularly storm-filled night during late 1886. While lightning scratched across the windows and wind howled off the harbor, Kienzy's guests became unusually subdued. Life had been tough on the group. Approaching winter hardened their thoughts. Suddenly, the door flew open, revealing a chilled and drenched comrade, George Leavenworth. The twenty-seven-year-old former Norwalk resident was a highly regarded newspaperman. Looking about the shadowy taproom, Leavenworth realized that not even the inviting fireplace could disguise the uneasy silence. The journalist laughed about his fellows' dire complexions and jokingly tossed out the idea that they appeared ready to form a Suicide Club, like the one Robert Louis Stevenson had written about a few years before. The young scrivener mused aloud, "Forming such a club would be good for news."

The men looked up at Leavenworth: "What's this? Explain yourself." A discussion ensued regarding what sort of membership requirements a Suicide Club might demand. Certainly such a society would be open to anyone tired of life. The members of the organization would gather as often as they wished, but it made sense to officially meet once a year, when an individual would be selected to kill himself. As the conversation grew more intense, a witness claims that Leavenworth broke into grisly song:

We meet 'neath the sounding rafter
And the walls around are bare;
As they echo our peals of laughter,
It seems that the dead are there.

Then stand by your glasses steady,
This world is a world of lies;
Here's a health to the dead already,
Hurrah for the next that dies.

Brightened with this banter about death, the men lifted their steins at Kienzy's. Leavenworth drew up a constitution and bylaws. A game of chance was needed, and poker was determined the best way to choose the unlucky victim; however, instead of cards, dice would be tossed. It was decided that each member would be allotted three throws, with the lowest hand named winner. One of the men seated at the table guffawed, "You mean loser. That's the poor chap who'll have to do himself in." The horrible game was set in motion. That night, the dice did not favor Victor Heisterhagen.

Heisterhagen was a highly regarded musician. For a decade, he served in the army band while stationed on Governors Island in New York City. Living in Bridgeport, he performed with popular sewing machine factory bands, first with the supremely talented Wheeler & Wilson Band and, more recently, with the Howe outfit. During the autumn of 1886, just about the time Heisterhagen tossed the cursed dice that howling night, the musician discovered that he suffered from a serious tooth disease. To his dismay, his playing career would soon vanish. Heisterhagen saw how well Bridgeport's pubs were doing and approached his friend and landlady, Mrs. Kate Gregory, for a loan with which to open a saloon. The musician-turned-tavern keeper was proud of his place in the Kusterer Block at 19 Gold Street, a few doors down from the boardinghouse where he resided. It became obvious, however, that, lacking steady clientele, his business teetered on failure after just a few months. Kate badgered Heisterhagen to repay the loan before he went completely broke. Neither his father back in Germany nor his well-to-do grocer brother in New Jersey came to Heisterhagen's financial aid. At 8:30 a.m. on February 3, 1887, Victor Heisterhagen opened the bar for the day. He took a step into the saloon's basement and closed the door behind him; a moment later, a pistol shot was heard. Kate found the musician slumped at the base of the stairs; Heisterhagen had shot himself in the right temple.

News of Heisterhagen's death sparked rumors that perhaps the morbid meeting at Kienzy's did actually form a suicide association. Was it a joke when the musician's death announcement referred to him as the club's vice-president? The notion of such a lethal society was too far-fetched to believe; rational voices around Bridgeport dismissed the gruesome idea.

Strangely, lacking any premeditation, on the anniversary of the suicide club's founding the surviving members returned, one by one, to John Kienzy's saloon. Compelled by some unseen hand, the dice were retrieved, and again the morbid bones were thrice tossed. The contest this evening claimed William Meckel. A common web now seemed to weave its way through the suicide club; aside from their Germanic roots, somehow, inexplicably, the secret society's influence seemed to especially touch certain downtown streets—a radius running east and west between Water and Main and north and south from Gold to Bank.

Meckel's wife had recently passed away. Now, as his business soured, he was evicted from his shop located on Wall Street. An attack of malarial fever was all that was needed to push the painter beyond coping. The forty-five-year-old thrust an ice pick twice into his chest; a rib deflected the pointed instrument away from his heart. Barely conscious, he slit his throat with a straight razor. Poor William agonized for three days before expiring on April 27, 1888.

Meckel's demise frightened the friends and family of remaining club members. They demanded that the boneyard seekers abandon their oaths and leave the society. Confrontations with outsiders had the club members denying that any such organization existed. However, one German American from West Stratford admitted that he had indeed withdrawn from the very real suicide club. This defector stirred the bile of surviving members; they dubbed the man a worthless coward.

Less than half a year later, on October 9, 1888, George E. Leavenworth, the talented newspaperman, drank an overdose of laudanum, a potent derivative of opium. He had moved to Bridgeport from his birthplace in Bethel, via Norwalk, in 1875. Hired as an apprentice for the *Bridgeport Evening Farmer*, George spent four years learning the printer's trade and quickly rose to the position of chief city editor. Wearied by deadlines and demands, Leavenworth left the profession in December 1887 but returned to journalism as night editor for the *Bridgeport Morning News* two weeks prior to his untimely death. No one could fathom why such a dynamic and extremely well-liked young man, one of the most popular bachelors in town, would commit suicide. Some blamed alcohol abuse; others close to Leavenworth noted a history of depression. Extreme pain caused by facial neuralgia was the reason for his possessing laudanum. George Leavenworth accomplished his final act in a rented room at Case's Hotel on Bank Street, well within the zone of the suicide club's supernatural grip.

Proceedings of the Suicide Club were kept in the strictest secrecy—that is, until John Kienzy, the expert marksman, shot himself in his basement. Kienzy had sold off his saloon and journeyed to Europe for health reasons. In Switzerland, he acquired two tons of specialty fromage and returned to Bridgeport with the hopes of becoming a cheese monger. The venture went bust, and the former pub owner decided to place a rifle to his chest, attach a taunt string and pull the trigger. It was rumored that Kienzy was president of the Suicide Club at the time. With his death, the *Bridgeport Evening Farmer* heralded that the city was home to a demonic suicide cluster, although some readers credited the article as merely the ginger work of zealous journalists trying to hawk newspapers. With Kienzy's passing, the members of the Suicide Club relocated their meetings to the Union Hotel, a popular German American resort. Situated on Water Street just north of the Atlantic Hotel, the three-story building was owned by George Wagner. Formerly, George's father had managed the place as the Wagner House. Under the younger Wagner's tutelage, the establishment cultivated a high regard in theatrical circles as far away as New York City. Audiences from across the region clamored for the hotel's summer garden and were entertained with lively vaudeville acts, booming brass oompah bands and twirling polka dancers—an ironic spot for meetings of the Suicide Club.

Following the organization's initial meeting on that stormy night at Kienzy's saloon in 1886, members strictly adhered to club edicts, selecting a single victim and then doing away with themselves at a pace of one person within every twelve months. The reality of this society's sad harvest compelled remaining acolytes to continually troll among Bridgeport's despondent citizens for new recruits; only secrecy and a willingness to obey the club's deadly dictates were necessary for initiation. Ensuing years never lacked sad individuals searching for, and fulfilling, self-destruction. One prospective convert was letter carrier William H. Maby. But just before the forty-seven-year-old's official induction into the morose brethren, Maby slit his throat with a razor on January 31, 1890. His wife's fight with insanity and her recent reinstitutionalization, along with his own ongoing struggles with insomnia, were viewed as the causes for Maby's sorrowful mental state.

At the mailman's funeral, he was mourned by fellow postal workers with a floral arrangement shaped as a four-foot-tall section of a lamp post. An attached flower mailbox read, "His Last Trip." Residents along the beloved postman's route commissioned another flower arrangement shaped as a three-foot-long envelope, adorned with a colorful bouquet postage stamp. The envelope's petal-drawn address listed "Our Faithful Carrier." Poignantly, the mailman had bequeathed a rather unique artifact to Bank Street resident Wendell Baum, the Suicide Club's secretary: a handsome silk umbrella. The fancy accoutrement's carved handle gruesomely displayed a scorpion gnawing on a human skull. Baum expressed an instant fascination with the morbid object and ostentatiously carried it wherever he ventured.

The next annual meeting of the Suicide Club determined that the owner of the skull-festooned umbrella would die. Baum had recently left his position as proprietor of a Bank Street boardinghouse and bar (called the New Haven House) and traveled to New York City, where he hoped to open a similar business. A friend recalled afterward Baum dropping hints about killing himself. The middle-aged German sardonically lifted his umbrella so everyone could get a closer inspection, stating, "A cloud hangs over me, I am doomed." Baum announced that his friends would probably attend his funeral within a week. The big city was uninviting to the former Bridgeport hotel owner. A spring rain fell as Baum meandered to a vacant lot at the foot of East Seventy-second Street, where he calmly removed a razor from his pocket and gashed his throat three times.

Despite these deaths, people across Connecticut, and indeed the nation, looked upon the existence of a Suicide Club as an unbelievable fiction. For three years it was reasoned that these tragic killings were a matter of coincidence; suicide was near epidemic in proportions during the late nineteenth century. The reality of such a secret society had been debated in Bridgeport newspapers and argued by Park City residents ever since rumors of the club first arose, but definitive proof had always been elusive. That is, until an early May afternoon during 1890, when a peculiar letter from Caen, in northwestern France, arrived at the Bridgeport Post Office. Seeing the lurid address prickled the hair on the back of everyone's neck who touched the envelope:

Monsieur
Le President du Suicide Club
Bridgeport,
Angleterre

Four Frenchmen, having experienced substantial business failures, decided to end their misery and join the Bridgeport Suicide Club. Inadvertently, they sent their letter to England, where the British postal service forwarded it to Connecticut. A letter carrier was dispatched to scour downtown inquiring who might claim ownership. Once word of the letter's arrival hit the streets, the public anxiously leered at each doorway the mailman entered, wondering who might retrieve the letter. Shock rippled through the city when a popular jeweler claimed ownership. It was watchmaker Daniel Loeser. For the first time, a person openly expressed membership in the Suicide Club. He bluntly stated that he was the organization's secretary and that he would deliver the letter to the proper, undisclosed president.

The existence of the Suicide Club was debated around the world. Some felt the entire concept was nothing but a morbid joke—until a letter from France arrived at the Bridgeport Post Office. *Courtesy of the Connecticut State Library.*

Watchmaker Dan Loeser was a respected Bridgeport resident loved by all. Rumors, however, indicate his dark side and a lurid connection to a rare "13 Club." *Courtesy of the Connecticut State Library.*

Everyone knew Dan was active in German musical societies across Connecticut and that he enjoyed flaunting his humorous disposition. The happy-go-lucky fellow famously won best costume category at the 1880 Germania masquerade ball held in New Haven. He also had a serious side, fighting for workers' rights.

Was Loeser playing along with a lurid joke that grew out of control, or did someone put him up to this stunt? The jeweler wouldn't answer. The letter's contents remained secure, too; as Loeser put it, "By request of the families of deceased members the full translation would not be divulged." Apparently, Bridgeport's Suicide Club was not a figment of anyone's savage imagination.

Marching into the new century, only two club members lingered. George Wagner, the owner of the Union Hotel, eventually did die of his own volition in 1904. He journeyed to New York City, spent an evening wandering Union Square and then proffered a German five-mark note to rent a room at a nearby hotel. Wagner's only luggage was two revolvers. In his first attempt to kill himself, investigators noted, the hammer merely clicked on the lone cartridge but did not fire. His wife felt that financial difficulties forced George to place the second pistol to his temple.

Wagner's death forced Dan Loeser, the sole remaining Suicide Club member, to confess that there was no such organization; the Suicide Club was a myth spawned by Loeser himself as a prank. The only thing was, in his statements following Wagner's suicide, Dan provided disinformation. He claimed he had sparked the ruse fifteen years before, in 1889; the club had already been in existence since 1886. Jovial Dan died of natural causes at the age of fifty-four during the first week of April 1905—curiously, about the same time of year the club had supposedly held its annual secret gatherings.

The last known rendezvous of the Suicide Club reportedly occurred at the Union Hotel on Water Street. Even after the organization's demise, guests here were escorted to rooms exclusively by candlelight for fear they would kill themselves using the gas fixtures. *Courtesy of the Connecticut State Library.*

The Union Hotel's popular vaudeville acts and summer beer garden had long fallen silent, but the Suicide Club's dark legacy lingered. The place had cultivated a bad reputation; there was something amiss about the Union. People crossed the street rather than walk within the hotel's shadow. A morbid fungus seemed to pulsate within the hotel's walls, beckoning the inconsolable to the Suicide Club's former lair. Even after the death of the noxious association, despondent individuals continued to lose their path in life only to find their way up the lonely stairs of the old establishment. During the turn of the twentieth century a number of persons, including a Bridgeport city clerk, signed their names to the hotel register destined to leave the Water Street hostelry in a coffin. The situation became so perverse that during the summer of 1907, the latest proprietor of the Union Hotel, Oscar E. Schroeder, would only send guests to bed by candlelight; too many suicides were being committed by residents using the suites' gas fixtures. When Schroeder collapsed dead on the sidewalk just four months afterward, people blamed the incident on a curse associated with the hoodoo hotel.

What was it that first brought members of the Suicide Club together that stormy night? If one had the opportunity to ask those gentlemen present at Kienzy's saloon or Wagner's if the secret society really existed, their reply most assuredly would have been a bitter grin. But just to be safe, in retrospect, it'd be best to shun those locales. Much to the chagrin of teetotaler P.T. Barnum, there were plenty of other bars in Bridgeport.

Graves, Ghouls
and the World's Greatest Showman

1891

They are neither man nor woman—
They are neither brute nor human—
They are Ghouls.
—Edgar Allan Poe, "The Bells," 1848

Phineas Taylor Barnum certainly strutted through life in the glow of the bizarre. From promoting Joice Heth, the 161-year-old (living!) nurse of baby George Washington, to exhibiting the mummified Feejee Mermaid, it becomes increasingly obvious just how much the "World's Greatest Showman" was the exemplar of nineteenth-century humbug gone wild. But his blatant huckstering also led some to peg the entertainer a shameless fraud. No matter, for as long as the public was talking about Barnum, in his mind, it amounted to free publicity.

One line of work that Barnum never would have wished to be associated with was the abhorrent profession of "ghoul." However, a close examination of the pitchman's political career scandalously connects him to grave desecration. The morbid results haunted Barnum during his later years and, in fact, followed him literally into, and almost out of, his own tomb. Shortly after the circus maven's death, at age eighty, something very unusual occurred at his graveside. Newspapers across the nation debated what may or may not have transpired in Bridgeport's Mountain Grove Cemetery. Barnum's associates and friends professed that evidence pointed a skeletal finger toward the midnight labors of grave robbers. On the other hand, the showman's parade of detractors suspected yet another well-planned, albeit lurid, publicity hoax. Whichever the case, the sepulchers of Mountain Grove, a cemetery Barnum himself helped found, witnessed "something" eerie during the early morning hours of May 29, 1891.

Born on July 5, 1810, Barnum abandoned such middle-class entrepreneurial ventures as store owner and newspaper editor in his hometown of Bethel, Connecticut, to follow an extravagant life touring the world with the "Swedish Nightingale," Jenny Lind, and the legendary Tom Thumb. When Barnum wasn't crowing before the crowned heads of Europe, he was legitimizing American theater, popularizing baby pageants and successfully attaining office as a four-term Connecticut state legislator, not to mention hosting museums of curiosities and circus realities. There was apparently nothing the marketing genius Barnum could not undertake and overwhelm.

Following illustrious careers that brought him riches and bankruptcies, the internationally toasted showman suffered a stroke in early November 1890. Sequestered in Marina, his palatial home on Bridgeport's shorefront, Barnum's health slowly deteriorated. On the evening of April 7, 1891, the emblem of populist democracy and one of America's best-known sons drew his final breath.

According to the *Hartford Courant*, Barnum's "expressed desire was to have the funeral as quiet as possible." Services were conducted without ostentation. Businesses were closed, buildings were draped with dark bunting and flags flew at half-mast. Droves of Bridgeport's reverent citizenry lined the streets for the funeral procession. When the mourners' rendition of "Auld Lang Syne" wafted out from the Second Congregational Church (also known as South Church), an emotional tidal wave rolled across the industrial city. Thousands more viewed the final procession leading from South Church along the two-mile route to Mountain Grove Cemetery.

The solemn day was not without vulgar incident. "Crooks always follow a circus," the *Bridgeport Sunday Herald* reported. When the Barnum & Bailey festivities were postponed at Madison Square Garden out of reverence for Mr. Barnum (P.T., incidentally, had also created this New York venue), thieves boarded Bridgeport-bound trains to ply their trade. Plainclothes policemen arrested four pickpockets outside the overflowing church as hymns of Whittier and Holmes were sung.

Celebrated showman and marketing entrepreneur Phineas Taylor Barnum (1810–1891) introduced theatrics and curiosities to audiences around the globe. His circus legacy continues to this day. However, few recall the macabre attempt to steal his corpse. *Courtesy of the Library of Congress, LC-DIG-cwpbh-02176.*

Barnum was buried beside his first wife, Charity, and other members of the Barnum clan. The Connecticut Yankee's final resting place was engineered to remain secure for eternity. The crypt lay within an eight-inch brick wall covered by a two-ton stone slab. "This kind of a grave,"

From acquiring London Zoo's beloved elephant, Jumbo, to his many real estate dealings, businessman Barnum amassed a bevy of detractors. Barnum's statue at Bridgeport's Seaside Park was slathered with unflattering graffiti during 1893, and in 1896, Barnum's grave site, illustrated here, was desecrated. Was this the work of idle hands or long-smoldering vengeance? *Courtesy of the Bridgeport Public Library, Bridgeport History Center.*

according to the Middletown, Connecticut *Penny Press*, "was made in accord with Barnum's wish, he having said that it was safer and that it could not be entered without attracting the attention of the watchmen of the cemetery." The People's Showman knew how to stun masses around the globe; apparently, he anticipated what could transpire on earth while he resided in the next world as well.

Following his interment, the April 13, 1891 *New York Times* ran an enigmatic article addressing a "rumor...that an attempt had been made to steal the remains of the late P.T. Barnum." This inaccurate, though prophetic, account resulted from the announcement that two special policemen, "one of them in uniform," were being stationed at the cemetery "to prevent," as the *Bridgeport Evening Farmer* reported, "vandals and relic hunters from stripping the grave of its floral adornments." The April 13 *Evening Farmer* painted a raucous picture of events at the funeral:

> *Even while prayers were being said at the grave, it was necessary to use force to prevent persons from crowding through the group of mourners and appropriating the flowers. Women whose attire and appearance would indicate that they had an ordinary respect for the dead and a regard for common decency, rushed forward and scooped up flowers with both hands, exhibiting the most astonishing boldness and indifference to the opinion of those present.*

The newspaper opined, "It was a sight to occasion wonderment and disgust." Absconding with casket wreaths was the least of the Barnum family's concerns. The *Evening Farmer* also made allusion to armed guards being positioned during the night to circumvent any "efforts that might be made to steal the body and hold it for a ransom as was done in the case of A.T. Stewart." Alexander Stewart, the multi-millionaire "Merchant Prince of Manhattan," had died in 1876. Two years later, for motives never determined, his body was stolen from St. Mark's churchyard in New York City and never recovered. The crime remains unsolved to this day.

Once the bunting was furled, flags raised and guards posted at the cemetery, Bridgeport was left to wrestle sadly with a post-Barnum world. Residents still anticipated a visit by the circus, and newspapers focused on the dedication of P.T.'s bronze visage modeled by Thomas Ball. The statue, already cast and waiting in a New Jersey warehouse for the granite base and steps to be constructed at Seaside Park, depicted Bridgeport's adopted son writing meditatively in an easy chair. Evidently, the showman's enemies wouldn't allow even his image a moment's repose. Within a week of its dedication in 1893, under cover of night, individuals assaulted the seated Barnum, covering the pedestal and steps with "uncomplimentary inscriptions" poignantly scrawled in red. The *Bridgeport Evening Post* denied that any vandalism occurred, stating that the story's unknown source was "possessed of a very brilliant imagination."

Controversy continued to hound Barnum following his demise. Just a month and a half after his burial, on May 29, 1891, at roughly 11:00 a.m., an individual stopped by the editorial offices of the *Evening Farmer* to voice concerns over the goings-on he had witnessed earlier that morning. The man, whom the newspaper refused to identify, reported that just shy of 2:00 a.m., while riding horseback near the entrance of Mountain Grove Cemetery, he heard a series of gunshots, probably half a dozen in all, emanating from within the graveyard. The lone rider leaned into the misting night trying to discern any further noises. Greeted by silence, he chalked the incident up to the actions of a cantankerous drunk stumbling home.

At first, staff at the *Farmer* dismissed the man's testimony, but the witness's adamant demeanor compelled a reporter to visit Barnum's personal secretary, Henry E. Bowser, and Charles R. Brothwell, the showman's agent and confidant. Barnum's advisers laughed a bit too heartily at the suggestion of something odd occurring at the famed man's final resting place. Undeterred, the reporter promised next to visit the

Charles R. Brothwell was a close personal assistant to P.T. Barnum. Reluctant at first to divulge information regarding the attempted grave robbery, Brothwell eventually admitted awareness of the crime. *Courtesy of the Connecticut State Library.*

graveyard, compelling Brothwell to shout, "Hold on! You're bound to find out anyhow…There has been an attempt to steal Mr. Barnum's body."

Earlier that same morning, Barnum's grave watchers, George Callahan and John Blakeman, had rushed into their superior's office and shared a chilling story. Beneath three large oaks, the guards lay asleep in a shanty situated about one hundred feet south of the tomb. Callahan and Blakeman apologized for their lax behavior, explaining that the string of uneventful nights had made them feel the grave site was safe, especially with the weather so drizzly. The cemetery watchmen were mistaken. At two o'clock in the morning, the men were startled from their sleep. Certain that he had heard the scrapings of a pick, Callahan roused his partner and cautiously approached the Barnum crypt. The sounds of digging were now unmistakable. Straining their eyes into the shadows, the guards drew their revolvers. Wrapped within the mist, silhouettes busily tossed dirt to one side of the tomb. Callahan shouted, "Who's there?" The phantom workers froze. Callahan and Blakeman discerned three figures: two men wielding tools, while a third steadied a lantern outside the hole. One of the apparent resurrectionists broke the hush with a startled exclamation. The lantern's beam turned on the guards and was extinguished abruptly. Callahan called out again. When no one replied, the guards fired a warning shot in the air. The ghouls dodged between gravestones, racing toward the cemetery pump, where a covered wagon waited.

Coverage in the *Middletown Penny Press* stated that upon emptying their pistols, either Callahan or Blakeman wounded one of the intruders. The three men fled with their tools, leaping into the secreted wagon driven by a fourth accomplice, and galloped away. Unsure if others lay in ambush among the tombs, Blakeman and Callahan broke their pursuit and retraced muddy steps searching for evidence. Adjacent to the Barnum crypt's western side, the guards discovered a shallow trench about one foot deep and four feet long. Atop the discarded sod lay a tin lamp commonly found aboard vessels; known as a "dark lantern," its sliding panel was used to produce a single beam of light.

After hearing Callahan and Blakeman's breathless testimony, Brothwell went to the police. Mrs. Barnum subsequently doubled the number of guards, who were instructed to shoot "at once" any body snatchers. Hundreds of very public daylight ghouls visited the cemetery gawking at nothing more than the filled-in handiwork of the would-be grave robbers.

Naturally, over the course of the next couple of days, citizens and journalists advanced theories as to who might have disturbed the Barnum plot. The most popular assumption was that shameless ghouls had plotted to secure Barnum's earthly remains for ransom. The macabre work of resurrection men was not so far-fetched an occurrence during the nineteenth century. Graves were secretly opened in search of valuables, and cadavers were illegally obtained by "sack-'em-ups" for medical students. Just a few years hence, the Secret Service would thwart an attempt to steal Abraham Lincoln's body in a scheme set on exchanging the president's corpse for money and a prisoner release.

Most locals considered grave robbing the only plausible reason for the nighttime cemetery visitation, an opinion often cited in Barnum biographies. Historian A.H. Saxon, author of the superb biography *P.T. Barnum: The Legend and the Man*, subscribes to the theory that grave robbers were responsible, noting that "city residents and Barnum's secretary, Bowser, who had recently taken to carrying a pistol, were in no doubt about [the veracity of the guards' story]."

Others were not so convinced. Contemporaries familiar with the showman's predilection for the sensational felt the whole incident was a hoax concocted by friends to highlight the circus coming to town. "No Clue as Yet," a May 30, 1891 follow-up article about the attempted grave pilfering, appeared

Resurrection men broke into graves and robbed corpses for their valuables, to ransom the remains or to sell the bodies to medical schools for experimentation. This illustration depicts the ghoulish crime taking place during the late nineteenth century somewhere in the vicinity of New York City. Frank Leslie's Illustrated Newspaper, *April 18, 1868; Michael J. Bielawa Collection.*

in the *Bridgeport Evening Farmer* and stated that Brothwell and Bowser were certain "that the attempt was genuine and only the presence of the guard[s] prevented the theft of the body." The article conveniently ran adjacent to a column announcing that same day's arrival of the Barnum & Bailey Circus in Bridgeport. The *Hartford Courant* announced that the graveside tale "Smacks of Advertising"; the *Bridgeport Daily Standard*'s brief observation was entitled "Not Generally Credited"; and the *New York Tribune* dubbed the incident merely "Silly Rumors." The *Bridgeport Sunday Herald* wagged an unequivocal finger: "A shameful fake was foisted upon a gullible world at the expense of the late P.T. Barnum." Editors termed the story "one of the most transparent hoaxes that ever was perpetrated." Supporting this view, it turns out, is the fact that Brothwell never did report the grave desecration to local police.

Another theory centers on the fact that Callahan and Blakeman's final day of employment was approaching. The guards themselves, some postulated, staged the extravagant incident to ensure a job extension. Still, individuals familiar with Callahan and Blakeman expressed the opinion that the guards were upstanding citizens incapable of fostering such a ruse.

Lacking any tangible leads, interest in the crime quietly waned. The circus arrived in town and moved on to New Haven, where, as tradition dictated, Yale students bombarded the parade marchers with skyrockets. Time passed. The story of Barnum's attempted grave robbery was forgotten. The legend became a footnote buried in history.

Well over one hundred years later, upon revisiting contemporary newspapers and, of all the unlikely sources, state law books, another chapter regarding the strange events at Mountain Grove Cemetery comes to light. This theory has never been articulated until now and is immersed in the coldest of motives: revenge.

During July 1873, perhaps through Barnum's influence, a special law was passed by the State of Connecticut calling for the closure of the old Bridgeport and Stratfield Burying Ground. The cemetery, dating from about 1811, was originally far removed from any homes or businesses on Division Street, today's Park Avenue. The last of an estimated four thousand burials took place there sometime during the 1850s. In the interim, the city had expanded, encircling the now overgrown and neglected graveyard. It did not go unnoticed that P.T. Barnum owned land adjacent to the Bridgeport and Stratfield Burying Grounds.

Between 1870 and 1872, more than half of the plot owners exchanged their burial lots for sites within the newer Mountain Grove Cemetery. The 1873 state statute explained that due to fading financial support, "interest in

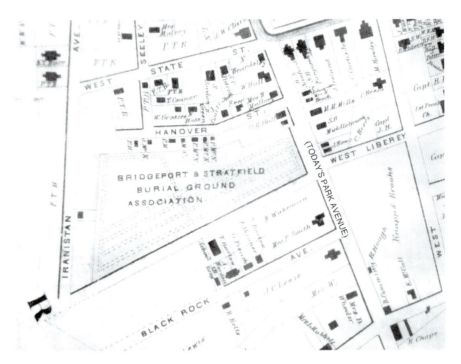

Old Bridgeport and Stratfield Burying Grounds, 1867. Decrepit and little used by the mid-nineteenth century, a state law authorized the relocation of remains interred here. The botched removals littered Bridgeport streets with bones and gravestones. *Courtesy of the Bridgeport Public Library, Bridgeport History Center.*

[the Bridgeport and Stratfield Burying Grounds] will be lost, and all revenue from which the fences could be maintained and the grounds kept in such order…will cease, and they will become a disgrace, discredit, and nuisance." It was therefore resolved by the state assembly to "remove the remains of all those persons deposited in the [olden] grounds…and the monuments erected over the same, and to re-deposit such remains in such suitable lots and grounds in the Mountain Grove Cemetery."

David W. Sherwood, a Barnum operative and board member of Mountain Grove Cemetery, agreed to cover costs for the removal and reinterment of all the Park Avenue graves. In return, Sherwood was to receive ownership of the old cemetery property. The expense proved too much for Sherwood. Ever so thoughtful, Barnum provided his friend with the financial means to complete the work, thus acquiring half the cemetery's lands for himself.

Not everyone was pleased with the new law or Barnum's land grab. Old guard families resented being ordered to rouse ancestors from their eternal slumber. The controversy came back to goad Barnum during his successful 1875 run for city mayor, forcing candidate Barnum to respond (in an unsigned editorial letter), "It was no unusual thing for burial grounds to be removed from the heart of a city."

But the most grievous complaints arose from just how the grave removals were unsanctimoniously conducted during 1873 and 1874. Barnum hired George Poole, a retired butcher who once worked at a Main Street meat market, to oversee the exhumation and transport of earthly remains and monuments. Bridgeport resident Julian H. Sterling, a longtime correspondent for the *New York World* whose family had slung barrels of ink back and forth with Barnum, expounded on how indecently the old cemetery was treated: "The dead were taken up in cartloads and carried, mostly at night time, to another resting place. The bodies were

American folk hero P.T. Barnum is buried in Mountain Grove Cemetery in Bridgeport. According to his wishes, Barnum's remains were placed within a thick brick crypt beneath a two-ton stone slab. Was this Barnum's attempt to thwart an anticipated grave robbery? *Courtesy of Michael J. Bielawa.*

reburied in the far side of Mountain Grove cemetery, monuments were broken, headstones replaced, and in many instances headstones were utilized for flagging side-walks about town." It's important to note that the "far side" of the burial grounds was located in the western section of Mountain Grove Cemetery. This fact will have a bearing on future events. An anonymous 1897 *New York Sunday World* article detailed how "sixteen and twenty [bodies] at a time were loaded on trucks and in broad daylight hauled by horses through the streets…Many of the graves were so old that the coffins were decayed or entirely gone. Some burst open and bones were scattered along the causeway."

Upon completion of the grave removals, the area encompassing the old Bridgeport and Stratfield Burial Grounds, now owned by Sherwood and Barnum, was laid out as a middle-class neighborhood. The profit Barnum generated in sales from bungalows and cottages lining the new Cottage Street, according to the *Sunday World*, was "more than a million dollars." By 1885, all evidence of the decrepit cemetery had been obliterated. That is, all the *above*-ground vestiges.

The removal of the dead was so badly handled that skeletal remains left behind were regularly uncovered whenever street excavations took place in the area. Throughout the closing decades of Bridgeport's nineteenth century, local newspapers commonly reported coffins, bones and broken headstones being exposed. Portions of city sidewalks, uprooted as recently as 1982 and 2000, have turned out to be inverted gravestones linked to the unethical practices of Mr. Poole. Considering the number of families affected by the closure of the Bridgeport and Stratfield Burying Grounds, and the outrageous treatment of their dead, it isn't difficult to imagine a handful of distraught descendants swinging a midnight pickaxe in order to provide P.T. Barnum with a little graveyard comeuppance. With no intention whatsoever of stealing the showman's body, perhaps a group of bluebloods removed a few clods of earth and heaped insult upon Phineas. By scratching a shallow trench on the western side of Barnum's grave, which faced the site where the Bridgeport and Stratfield remains had been reinterred, these mock ghouls and their intentionally abandoned dark lantern most likely desired only to spotlight the dishonor to their families.

Controversial all these years later, and from the afterlife to boot, Barnum smiles still over the free publicity. Ever the showman of the unnatural, Phineas Taylor Barnum continues to bask within the bizarre.

LEGEND OF THE BRIDGEPORT AND STRATFIELD BURYING GROUNDS

Long before the Bridgeport and Stratfield Burying Grounds became a shunned location and its marble tombstones were unceremoniously removed, a strange mystery inhabited the Division Street cemetery. Hushed whispers spoke of a tombstone inscribed with the birth and death dates of a twelve-year-old boy. The memorial itself was quite ordinary. However, what did compel townsfolk to marvel were the peculiar markings on the stone's *opposite* side. Customarily blank, the back of this particular grave marker depicted the outline of an adult female, half squatting, holding a weapon in her upraised hand. The headstone was visited by hundreds of residents over the years, but none could decipher its hidden meaning. No one could answer who, or what, may have been responsible for the disturbing etching. Out of decency for the child's eternal slumber, the gravestone was replaced three times. In each instance, the scratched tableaux of the angry woman reappeared. Commentary on this phenomenon was reported in an issue of the *Bridgeport Daily Standard* during the winter of 1870, which placed the boy's year of death at about 1835. The article tactfully pointed to locals who may have been covering up a murder. Thus, the supernatural appearance of the female outline may have been the young victim summoning justice from beyond the grave. Although the stone eventually vanished, perhaps the ghostly drawing still exists, like other Division Street gravestones, hidden just under the surface somewhere in Bridgeport.

The Invaders

1892

"It will be pure luck" should any of those responsible for Beardsley's death ever
be brought to justice.
—Bridgeport Standard, *January 3, 1893*

One of New England's greatest unsolved mysteries concerns the
murder of Bridgeport benefactor James W. Beardsley. For well over
a century, this crime has haunted the Park City, a community that owes
its nickname, in large part, to the magnanimous Mr. Beardsley. It was his
generosity that led to the creation of one of Connecticut's most magnificent
recreational areas, and most assuredly, contributed to his brutal death.

James Walker Beardsley was born in Monroe, Connecticut, about the
year 1820. As a young man, he inherited from an uncle, James Walker, a
sizable amount of land situated along Bridgeport's northern border. He
relocated here, living in the family's ancestral manse, built in 1739, where
three generations of Walkers and Beardsleys toiled, tilled and were buried.
A respected drover, Beardsley sold cattle to most of this area's butchers
until Midwest railroads usurped the New England beef market. Certainly,
during the Civil War, Beardsley's business as a cattle broker came at a time
when the Union army was in an ever-demanding need of meat. As earnings
increased, Beardsley expanded his agricultural ventures and became active
in the real estate market both within Bridgeport and out west in Illinois,
where he owned a sizable cattle ranch.

The rancher gradually acquired all the land along the eastern banks of
the upper Pequonnock River, as far south as the factory pond. These bucolic

James Beadsley, the man who helped create one of New England's greatest urban parks, was brutally murdered. The case has remained unsolved for over a century. *Courtesy of Connecticut's Beardsley Zoo, Bridgeport, Connecticut.*

rolling hills, sparkling river and rocky ledges teemed with wildlife, providing a glimpse of primeval Connecticut. From the pinnacle of Walker Hill, spectacular views were offered, not only overlooking Long Island Sound but, even more stunningly, northward into dense woodland. This was not only a wise investment on the part of Beardsley but, in fact, a hard-waged windfall of righteousness. Huge sections of the same property had once, during the eighteenth century, been held by his predecessors. Embracing these woodlands must have been a matter of great personal pride, like a Bridgeport variation of Emperor Justinian reclaiming Roman lands.

Long before the phrase "green space" entered the lexicon of politicians eager to slow New England's suburban sprawl, James Beardsley, in an absolute noble gesture, donated 125 acres of this land to the City of Bridgeport. The only stipulation Beardsley attached was that the area remain a public park. Squire Beardsley, esteemed farmer, cattleman and land baron, was dubbed a local hero. The City Common Council resolved in March 1878 "that the heartfelt thanks of the citizens of Bridgeport are due and are hereby, through their representatives, the common council of the said city, tendered to their fellow citizen, James W. Beardsley, for his magnificent gift to the city of a public park."

By age seventy-two, James was a well-known fixture in town. From his secluded country estate near the park bearing his name, Beardsley oversaw a business empire. The millionaire seemed busier than ever, what with planning the layout and plantings for the sprawling park. But it wasn't all work. He also posed for a series of photographs, adorned in frockcoat and vest, holding his hat and cane; the images would be used to cast a life-size bronze set to stand atop the park's scenic Walker Hill. Sadly, the generous cattle baron would not live to see the statue.

Old man Beardsley surely must have seemed the perfect mark for burglars plotting to rob his home just a few days before Christmas 1892. For these thieves, the only thing between a vast fortune and a quick getaway were the rich man's doddering sister, Julia, and Burr Oakley, a hired hand. But plans set into motion by the invaders on Thursday, December 22, took an icy twist, the outcome of which has remained a haunting question in the minds of city residents and park visitors ever since.

That first full day of winter, the doorbell of the Beardsleys' manor rang unexpectedly at 7:15 p.m. A social call at this hour was unusual for a home so far off the beaten path. When James answered the door, two masked men thrust themselves past him into the foyer. Their faces were disguised by white handkerchiefs. But old man Beardsley wasn't looking them in the eye; he was staring at the revolvers they grasped. "Don't be alarmed," the larger of the pair stated, "we don't intend to hurt you. What we want is your money."

Beardsley handed over sixty dollars he had withdrawn from the bank earlier that day, along with his prized pocket watch and chain. Told that there was no other money in the house, the thieves split up; one took the hired man, Burr Oakley, from room to room by candlelight, ransacking the place. The remaining burglar placed a gun to Beardsley's temple. Rifling through the various rooms proved that the homeowner was telling the truth; there was no money to be found. Disappointed, the thieves exited to the sound of wheels and gravel emanating from a waiting carriage, indicating that a third accomplice was involved. The entire affair took only twenty minutes.

Beardsley composed himself, checked on the condition of his sister, Julia, and asked the hired man to fetch a wagon. They sped south on Trumbull Road, past the location of the old tollgate, arriving at Police Chief John Rylands's office at about eight o'clock. The chief listened to Beardsley's tremulous voice and observed his anxious movements; obviously, the intruders had a deep effect on the old cattle rancher. A quick inquiry at local liveries revealed that a wagon had been rented by three strangers. Authorities hid at the stable of L.B. Sterling waiting for that particular jitney to be returned. At ten o'clock, nearly three hours following the robbery, three suspects were apprehended. During the subsequent police interview, one of the three out-of-towners explained that they had requested the vehicle for a ride into north Bridgeport, which happened to be Beardsley's neighborhood. The suspicious men were escorted to the scene of the crime for positive identification, whereupon two of the three were released. However, the third fellow created some consternation with old man Beardsley. He wasn't quite sure, but somehow he knew the suspect. Oakley reassured the old man that the fellow was from Easton and certainly had no ties to the robbery. Flummoxed, the constables released the final suspect.

With Christmas fast approaching, Bridgeport shoppers gathered outside downtown stores pondering who could have perpetrated such a bold robbery. A few days after the home invasion, an officer visited Beardsley in order to follow up on interviews; perhaps James, his sister Julia or Oakley had recalled something relevant to the case during the intervening time. The policeman stood shocked upon entering the sitting room. Beardsley was reclining on a couch, barely conscious, covered with poultices and plasters. The old man was gravely ill. In his wracked state, Beardsley could offer nary an objection, thus emboldening Julia to divulge what had really transpired on the evening of December 22.

That fateful night, while James was engrossed in his library (a marvelous collection of vellum-bound manuscripts and leather tomes), he was quite unaware that two burglars had entered his home. The masked intruders stumbled upon Julia in a room adjacent to the library. As they forced the seventy-six-year-old woman through a door leading to Beardsley and his books, the elderly cattle rancher rose from his desk to rescue his sister. James was throttled and thrown savagely into a chair and then onto the floor. One of the disguised assailants pinned the gasping old man down with a knee to the stomach.

Back at headquarters, officers wondered about the reluctance of Beardsley to bring these brutal facts to light. The rancher may have felt emasculated by being unable to stop the vandals. Probably the thieves threatened to return and kill everyone in the house should Beardsley confide what had transpired.

The millionaire's silence brought tragic results. Following the attack, he'd been seized by a debilitating nervous condition and bladder paralysis. The physician summoned to the Trumbull Road residence shook his head; James Beardsley was too far gone. Journalists reported he'd been "healthy and hale" prior to the robbery, but the thieves, who stole only a few belongings, had left behind an immobile old man, dying as a result of a merciless thrashing.

Tragically, one of Bridgeport's favorite citizens departed this world on New Year's Day 1893. As far as the law was concerned, these burglars were now also wanted for murder. Following Beardsley's death, Police Chief Rylands and local reporters again questioned the landowner's reluctance to state the truth about what occurred during the burglary. James initially explained that no one was harmed by the burglars and he and his sister merely obeyed demands after opening the door.

The answer may lie in a bizarre incident. Roughly four years earlier, while traipsing through woods belonging to Beardsley, a hunter discovered a cave-dwelling hermit. Word about the recluse enticed locals to visit the man, who had turned his back on the smokestacks and whirring engines of industrial Bridgeport. The notoriety was not appreciated. The hermit, nicknamed Snap Quigley, shunned attention, but the sheer number of curious residents pounding a path to his cave was damaging Beardsley's property. Shortly before the home invasion, the millionaire, along with a few hired men, visited the hermit. Quigley was forced from the cave, while his belongings were unceremoniously torched. The angered hermit stumbled away. But before vanishing into the forest, he turned and, with a raised fist, hurled a curse at Beardsley, finishing with the oath, "You will never die a natural death." It was said that during the remaining months leading to Beardsley's murder, the rich man was shaken to the point of despair by the hermit's venomous epithet.

Beardsley was buried in the family plot in the village of Nichols. The last will and testament of the man who made Beardsley Park a jewel of civic pride was read a month and a half later. News of the Beardsley estate and his financial holdings stunned the city. The landowner, whom so many residents had grown up knowing as fabulously wealthy, was nearly broke. It was popularly accepted that Beardsley's worth must have been at least $150,000. But when lawyers tallied his home, savings and livestock, it barely added up to $18,000. Beardsley really wasn't concealing any riches from the intruders.

As for solving the murder, authorities glumly admitted there were no leads. Lacking any specifics, reporters and officers alike resigned themselves to the scenario that "it'd be pure luck" should any of those responsible for Beardsley's death ever be brought to justice.

Surprisingly, luck did change. Just before three o'clock on the morning of March 1, 1894, fourteen months after Beardsley died, Officer Richard Larkin spotted a tiny glow floating from room to room in one of the city's posh residences while walking his rounds along State Street at the intersection of Park Avenue. That strange light emanated from the home of John M. Wheeler, founder of Wheeler & Howes Company, one of the state's largest dealers in coal and stonemason supplies. Wheeler's massive operation was located at the foot of the Congress Street Bridge, opposite downtown.

Someone was striking a match while roaming around the lower floors of the Wheeler place. Larkin approached the residence, hopped a fence and watched the gleam move upstairs. Cupping his eyes to the darkened first-floor windows showed nothing, but peering into the basement brought into view a man holding a candle descending the staircase. His face was covered with a silk cloth or handkerchief. A second intruder stood on the cellar stairs just out of sight. Concealing himself behind the hedges, Officer Larkin waited near the home's Park Avenue entrance. After a few minutes, hushed silhouettes filled the doorway. Larkin, unsure of how many bandits there were, ordered the men to throw their hands in the air. Twice, the unmistakable metal sounds of a cocked pistol clicked from the dark porch. Well hidden, Larkin pointed his revolver and pulled the trigger. His weapon did not misfire. Two gun blasts woke the Wheelers, who raced for the windows. They had slept through the intrusion due to the racket caused by a faulty furnace and convinced themselves that any noises heard that night were due to the heating device's rattling. Commotion filled the Wheelers' home and yard. Struggling back through the wooden doorframe, the bandits crashed into Victorian furnishings and decorations as they raced through the rooms. Larkin blew his piercing whistle, racing for the back of the house, as he figured the culprits would try to escape through the basement. As the crooks emerged from the hatch, Larkin ordered them back inside or he'd blast their heads off.

Responding to the whistle, Officers Hall and Leonard took positions around the house. At that same instant, Officer Hall bumped into Dr. George Skiff Ford, who had happened to be passing down the street, medical bag in hand, returning from a house visit. His presence looked mighty suspicious, considering the situation. In the cacophony, the cop thought Dr. Ford was one of the burglars, until Mrs. Wheeler, shouting from her bedroom window, informed the police of the physician's identity. The good doctor then joined the police guarding the Wheeler place. Figuring they were surrounded, two of the thieves surrendered. A third was discovered in the hallway, shot through the back. Stretched out and bleeding, a revolver at his side held a full complement of bullets, including two misfired rounds.

The captured men identified themselves as Joseph Corbett and William Henry, both of Louisville, Kentucky. Their partner, Edward Fitzsimmons of Chicago, lay mortally wounded in Bridgeport Hospital. Even after a successful operation removed the slug from the wounded man's spine, chances of survival were slim.

Justice was swift. One day after the failed heist, Corbett and Henry were brought before the local judge and admitted their guilt. Praying for lenience, they were shocked to be remanded to the Connecticut State Prison in Wethersfield for fifteen years. Upon hearing the punishment, Corbett wept

The shootout at the Wheeler house on the corner of State Street and Park Avenue netted desperate criminals wanted in three states. *Courtesy of the Connecticut State Library.*

like a child. It took a couple of days, but authorities did uncover the thieves' true identities.

By then, however, New York detectives investigating a string of robberies on Long Island had arrived in Bridgeport to question the hospitalized crook. It seems that the descriptions and methods employed by the men arrested inside the Wheeler home had a lot in common with an extensive list of burglaries occurring in and around Long Island City and Stockbridge, Massachusetts. Entering the hospital room, Detectives McCauliffe and O'Brien of the Long Island City force, and Officer White from Brooklyn, immediately recognized the bedridden fellow as Edward J. Fitzpatrick. Fitzpatrick realized the jig was up and hailed Officer White by his first name: "Hello, Christie!" The New York officers were left disappointed by not having an opportunity to personally confront the paralyzed thief's partners; the prison train had already departed Bridgeport that morning. Court photographs taken earlier that week, however, proved that "Henry" was, in truth, William Mahoney and that the convict calling himself "Corbett" was actually career criminal "Big Tom" Kinsella.

"Big Tom" Kinsella (right), alias Joseph Corbett, was the mastermind behind a Brooklyn crime ring; both he and seasoned burglar William Mahoney (left), alias William Henry, were persons of interest regarding the unsolved murder of James Beardsley. *Courtesy of the Connecticut State Library.*

The prisoner "Fitzpatrick" lying in a Bridgeport hospital bed was a onetime Long Island City constable. He'd been implicated in a Maspeth, New York home invasion that took place just two and a half months earlier (on December 22, 1893, the one-year anniversary of the Beardsley robbery). During the Maspeth heist, which netted thousands of dollars in diamonds, the thieves entered the palatial, adjoining mansions of the sugar merchant Meyer brothers, Christopher and Cord. The spacious homes of the elite New Yorkers were far removed from other residences. Christopher lived with his two elderly sisters, Elizabeth and Annie. That evening, the women had left their brothers at the Hanover Club, headed back home and retired to the room they shared. At 1:30 a.m., Elizabeth Meyer was startled awake when she discovered a man leaning over her. A candle and revolver were steadied in his right hand while he probed under her pillow with the left. When Annie noticed what was happening, she cried out, "Oh, don't kill us. Please don't harm us." The burglar with a heavy black mustache held them at gunpoint while other burglars rummaged through the mansion. He assured the sisters in a soothing New England accent, "Keep quiet.

Keep quiet and you shall not be harmed." The sisters believed that four intruders had entered the house and that a fifth was stationed outside. Two of the burglars wore dark cutaway coats and derbies. Both of their faces were disguised with silk handkerchiefs.

A week later, police staked out the Astoria Packinghouse on a tip that a robbery was planned. The New Year's Eve surveillance team caught three suspects: Edward Fitzpatrick, William Mahoney and Michael Sherlock. Authorities were certain that these men were part of the ring that had been pulling jobs around New York, including the Meyers' jewelry heist. Sadly, they were released due to a lack of evidence. In fact, the Long Island City detective force

Edward Fitzpatrick, shot during a Bridgeport robbery, died while in custody. The former Long Island City constable turned to a life of crime and likely knew James Beardsley's killer. *Courtesy of the Connecticut State Library.*

was so adamant about capturing the band dubbed the Masked Burglars that rival detectives, headlined as "jealous hawkshaws," arrested gang members too enthusiastically. All those innocent citizens dragged in front of the New York judge effectively catapulted these true culprits to freedom. As a result, the zealous gumshoes caused the detectives working as undercover plainclothesmen to get busted back to twirling nightsticks and walking a beat.

Now in Bridgeport, three suspects were caught red-handed. Turns out the men were part of the expansive Masked Burglars crime ring that preyed on wealthy homeowners across Long Island, western Massachusetts and in the Greater Bridgeport area. Kinsella was the hulking burglar who had been fingered as possessing the smooth voice and gentlemanly manners. In addition to the John M. Wheeler break-in, he was also implicated as having pilfered prominent families in neighboring Stratford. The gang was probably involved in two other attempted break-ins taking place in Bridgeport during the early hours of February 10, 1894: one involving Dr. Sidney Bishop's home (only the wife and her aunt were present) and the other taking place at the fabulous neo-gothic Nathaniel Wheeler Mansion on Golden Hill (only Mrs. Wheeler was home).

Wary of exposing their illegal labors in any single area, these crooks rotated from city mansions to country estates. An ongoing investigation, conducted by the Long Island City police, proved that there were at least five gang members still at large.

Following the failed John Wheeler break-in, the gang began to unravel. In April 1894, a month and a half after Fitzpatrick was shot and died, Michael Sherlock and Christopher Madden were arrested in New York City. Sherlock had been under surveillance during his visits to Stockbridge. Newspapers pointed at both Kinsella and Sherlock as being the "gentleman burglar" sneaking into affluent homes of the summer Berkshire community.

Inspired by these break-ins, Elizabeth Phipps Train penned the story "The Social Highwayman" for the July 1895 *Lippincott's Monthly Magazine*. This popular work was republished as a novel and then transformed into a Broadway play. Whether it was Sherlock or Kinsella addressing their Berkshire captives, it was apparent that the gang's point man always employed a soothing tact. Despite this beguiling approach, confrontations sometimes erupted. In one instance, according to the *New York Times* of September 10, 1893, Laura B. Field, in her Stockbridge bedchamber, refused to surrender a $1,200 watch. After his reassuring voice failed, the burglar "threw [the woman] forcibly against the wall…In her plucky fight the flesh of her hands had been torn in places, her arms were swollen and discolored, and her nightdress was in shreds."

The crime spree orchestrated by the Masked Burglars caused wealthy Bostonians and New Yorkers to vacate their breezy western Massachusetts idylls from the autumn of 1892 through 1893. When Sherlock and Madden were finally arrested because of their Berkshire activities, stories began circulating that these two criminals had also participated in, and neatly escaped, the thwarted Wheeler robbery in Bridgeport.

Sherlock stood at five feet, eleven inches and was remembered by his victims for his small hands. Another personal attribute nailed Sherlock on the witness stand. The streetcar

Michael Sherlock, once a New York City streetcar conductor, may have been the "Gentleman Burglar" of the Berkshires who inspired a novel and a Broadway play. *Courtesy of the Connecticut State Library.*

conductor turned burglar was identified by what female witnesses called his "soothing mesmeric voice." Christopher Madden was the physical opposite of Sherlock. Newspapers described his appearance as "hideous." A barroom brawler, part of Madden's lower lip was missing, bitten off during a fight six years earlier at Hogan's saloon, a favorite Long Island City haunt of the Masked Burglars. The fellow who claimed the bloody trophy, a rough-and-tumble newspaper editor, ended up dead shortly afterward. As for the recent string of home invasions, evidence lacked in connecting Madden to the Masked Burglars, so the brawny suspect was released. But Sherlock was transferred from New York to Massachusetts, where he would stand trial.

During the spring of 1894, well before Michael Sherlock stood in front of a judge, police from various communities visited the Connecticut State Prison attempting to coax information from Thomas Kinsella. Private detectives from the Pinkerton and McLaughlin agencies, as well as officers from Long Island, Bridgeport and Massachusetts, inquired, without success, what jobs the gang had pulled and where the missing loot was hidden. One detective even offered Big Tom $1,000, to be deposited in an outside bank account, should he come clean.

Amazingly, the key witness to step forth in the Sherlock case was Big Tom Kinsella's wife, Jennie. Destitute after living the high life, and bitter over other gang members kicking free, Jennie went to the coppers. Jennie's brother-in-law, George Fuller, was also in the masked gang. He burst into her apartment raving drunk, threatening to kill his wife, and then knocked Jennie around the flat. Fearing for her life, Jennie turned state's witness and "peached" on aloof gang members. Mrs. Kinsella painted quite a picture. She admitted that Big Tom was the gang's leader and that their Greenpoint, Brooklyn home was the staging area for the burglaries carried out on Long Island and in the Berkshires and Bridgeport. Jennie listed the band's hierarchy. Edward Fitzpatrick was second in command, and third in control was Michael Sherlock. This lippy goldmine led to the arrest of her brother-in-law, George Fuller, and the re-arrest of Christopher Madden. Jennie eagerly agreed to testify against Sherlock, who was under lock and key in Massachusetts. Madden, her testimony made clear, was usually positioned in a wagon outside the mansions as a lookout and to provide the gang's quick getaway. Jennie's talking also incriminated her brother, Michael Bannon, who was arrested for receiving stolen goods. Treading dangerous waters, Jennie Kinsella demanded police protection.

Four officers were detailed to keep an eye on Mrs. Kinsella's apartment, but the number quickly dropped to only one protector. Neighbors remarked that the guards were a farce; authorities overlooked huge, booze-fueled parties taking place at her apartment during all hours of the day and night. One resident remarked how sixty bottles of whiskey entered the flat over one particularly raucous forty-eight-hour period. Then, on July 19, 1894, the day before Jennie Kinsella was supposed to travel to Massachusetts and testify against Sherlock, she was found dead in her home. Suspicions obviously were raised, but the examining physician stated that Mrs. Kinsella passed away due to Bright's disease exacerbated by alcohol. The coroner quashed any

Saloon brawler Christopher Madden lost his lips during one particularly savage fight. *Courtesy of the Connecticut State Library.*

further investigation. As for Michael Sherlock, Jennie Kinsella's newfound silence had no bearing on his trial's outcome in Pittsfield, Massachusetts. The district attorney divulged William Mahoney's full Connecticut State Prison confession implicating Sherlock.

Mahoney's statements clearly illustrate that Big Tom was the boss and brains of the operation. Tom's violent side was portrayed, too. Mahoney related how the gang leader "threw the cripple [New Lenox, Massachusetts stationmaster and storekeeper Oscar Hutchinson] to the floor" and then "went after [Mrs. Hutchinson] when she emerged with a gun."

Sherlock, the former streetcar conductor, was found guilty and sentenced to fifteen years in the Massachusetts State Prison in Charlestown. With gang members either dead or incarcerated, the notorious Masked Burglars were effectively shut down. Their year-and-a-half reign of terror as the Northeast's most notorious crime ring ceased.

Striking similarities exist between the robberies conducted by Kinsella's gang and the Beardsley home invasion. Consider the modus operandi of the criminals:

- Mansions and summer wealthy retreats are targeted
- Prominent families are marked
- Familiarity with the layout of the grounds and schedules of homeowners
- Victims are often senior citizens
- Masked perpetrators
- Two+ men enter the home
- Manners of the gentleman burglar
- One burglar holds a family member(s) with a gun pointed at their head
- A second burglar is escorted through the house by family member/ servant
- An accomplice waits in a wagon outside the home
- Use of revolvers
- Jewelry/pocket watches and cash are stolen
- Items are pawned in New York
- Robbery locales rotate from Bridgeport to Long Island to western Massachusetts

But greater truth was forthcoming. Unresolved after nearly seven years, the Beardsley slaying reentered the public consciousness in a big way. On Wednesday, October 25, 1899, Park City residents awoke to a *Bridgeport Morning Union* headline screaming, "MURDER MYSTERY IS

SOLVED." Bridgeport police captain Eugene Birmingham always had suspicions regarding the Beardsley matter. He never faltered from his intuition about that robbery and the Wheeler home bandits having something in common. Now, he found himself in charge of the police department. During the autumn of 1899, the superintendent visited Wethersfield penitentiary and suddenly, somehow, the press obtained a confession regarding Beardsley's killing. Birmingham admitted that this confession lay in the basement of city hall, safely inside a vault at police headquarters. The story was repeated by the *Bridgeport Evening Farmer*, *New Haven Evening Register*, the *New York Sun* and the *Washington Evening Times*. Speculation indicated that one of the Masked Burglars, either Mahoney or Kinsella, had finally blabbed while sitting in the Connecticut big house. But which one?

The confession stated that before Christmas 1892, Thomas Kinsella and William Mahoney left their Brooklyn crime den for Bridgeport. They planned to rob a Christmas tree salesman named Green. Kinsella, for a while, had actually lived on Bridgeport's East Side. He knew about the Great Barrington farmer's annual holiday trek to the Park City. But the opportunity to confront Green at his shop on Housatonic Avenue never developed. Mulling other possible jobs, Kinsella grinned; he knew a rich old man who lived in an out-of-the-way part of town, just a bit north of the park. The wealthy coot stayed with his spinster sister and a butler.

On December 22, 1892, Julia Beardsley answered a knock at the side door. Before she could even gasp, Kinsella and Mahoney burst through the threshold and into New England crime history. James Beardsley sat in his library while Burr Oakley warmed himself beside the kitchen stove. Old man Beardsley rose to protect his sister. He refused to cooperate with the burglars, and Big Tom wrestled with the seventy-two-year-old man. In the struggle, the cattle rancher was tossed over a chair and eventually pinned to the floor by Kinsella's knee. Big Tom stayed with Beardsley and Julia, while Oakley was compelled at gunpoint to escort Mahoney through the house searching for valuables. When the hired man reappeared with Mahoney, Beardsley shouted at Oakley, "Get the dog!" Kinsella calmly responded, "You can't fool me. I know that you haven't got any dog." The burglars then entered the walk-in pantry, devouring all the pies they could find. Ever so politely, one pie was set aside, they explained, for their partner waiting in the wagon.

The thieves then made their way down the river and headed for Fairfield, where they followed the railroad tracks west to Norwalk. After a meal, they jumped an outbound freight, got into the Harlem yards and returned to Brooklyn. Beardsley's pocket watch was hocked at a pawnshop. The unnamed confessor explained that Fitzpatrick, the co-conspirator shot by Officer Larkin during the Wheeler invasion, "was not with us when we did the Beardsley job." In all likelihood, the man waiting in the wagon outside the Beardsley home was the burglars' regular lookout, Christopher Madden.

Was it Kinsella or Mahoney who finally confessed to authorities? The *Brooklyn Eagle* reported on October 26, 1899, that a veteran of the Bridgeport police force anonymously stated:

> *"The penitent thief is Kinsella." When asked how* [the police officer] *knew that, he said: "I have never lost track of the gang, for I didn't know when I might be called upon to be after them again. The reason I know who made the confession, if any confession was made, is because Kinsella is the only one of the gang now in Wethersfield prison. I know that Mahoney is reported to be dying in the prison hospital, but in reality he was pardoned several months ago and is now with relatives on Long Island. Sherlock was captured after the others were jailed and was convicted in Massachusetts of many burglaries, and he is now serving a long sentence there."*

However, the possibility that William Mahoney blabbed also has some grist to it. In all likelihood it was actually Mahoney, aka William Henry, who broke the silence. He spilled the beans on the gang during Sherlock's Pittsfield trial. Five years after his conviction for the failed Wheeler robbery, he became gravely ill with consumption. The bet was on that Mahoney offered a confession in return for freedom. In May 1899, he applied for a pardon due to health reasons, and on June 5, his request was granted with the help of Bridgeport attorney Jacob B. Klein. Conditions of his release stipulated that Mahoney's parents had to take custody of their son and remove the ex-con out of state to their Pennsylvania home. Confessor or not, something surely was afoot concerning Mahoney during that autumn of 1899. Inexplicably, a day after the Wethersfield prison confession hit newspapers, Mary Mahoney, William's protective sister, stopped by Bridgeport police headquarters for what turned into a heated argument with Superintendent Birmingham.

Did the document truly exist? Or was this just a clever ruse to startle Kinsella into really talking? The *Hartford Courant* flatly labeled the unseen confession, supposedly in Birmingham's safekeeping, a complete hoax. Interestingly, in December 1906, shortly before Big Tom's scheduled release from prison, another confession story entered Bridgeport's newspapers. The *Evening Farmer* announced, "Beardsley Murder Mystery Cleared Up by Confession," and the *Bridgeport Post* heralded, "Beardsley's Murderer Confesses." Once again, the document was supposedly locked in Superintendent Eugene Birmingham's vault, and Kinsella was named the killer. In this instance, the now deceased William Mahoney was definitely identified as the one who talked to the authorities. The consumptive confessor also allegedly claimed that neither Fitzpatrick nor Sherlock was present at the Beardsley robbery.

Over one hundred years after the crime, evidence finally points to Kinsella's Masked Burglars as perpetrating one of Connecticut's greatest unsolved murders. One of these men—Christopher Madden, Michael Sherlock, Thomas Kinsella, William Mahoney or Edward Fitzpatrick— most assuredly caused the death of James Beardsley. Two or more of the gang were accomplices to the bloody deed taking place that long-ago night of December 22, 1892. Who was the murderer? The most likely candidate is Tom Kinsella, the tall bandit leader with a penchant for manhandling his elderly victims. Big Tom controlled the gang, and he alone would have initiated a response to soften the belligerent Mr. Beardsley.

Maybe the day will come when, somewhere on a dusty shelf in the city's archives, or perhaps lying forgotten in the police department's property room, an age-stained letter will be brushed off, revealing the dying words of an ex-con's long-lost confession, proving for all time Beardsley's slayer.

"Big Tom" Kinsella

In and out of prison, responsible for the accidental killing of his mother-in-law, hard-drinking Tom Kinsella seemed to carry tragedy wherever he traveled. Thomas Kinsella Jr. was born in the small town of Stockbridge, Massachusetts, situated in the rolling Berkshires on the banks of the Housatonic River about 1857. The Kinsella brothers were regarded throughout the tightknit community as a rowdy handful. Tom and sibling James both saw time in the state reform school.

But punishment never deterred Thomas from running with the village's tough crowd. A stagecoach stop between Albany and Boston, Stockbridge attracted highwaymen. Rich in iron, the region was populated by miners and blast furnace workers stoked on free company whiskey. Charcoal burners, too, considered among the lowest rung of society, inhabited the hills surrounding the village. At age twenty-five, Tom served a prison term for larceny. He'd also escaped once from the Stockbridge jailhouse, and there was a warrant out for his arrest concerning a highway robbery when a defenseless man was savagely beaten.

Despite his criminal background, folks noted that Tom carried his well-proportioned five-foot, eleven-inch frame with a grace that made him appear taller. Perhaps this is the origin of his Big Tom moniker. Indeed, what his gentle, elegant voice couldn't convey to female admirers, Tom's blue eyes silently commanded.

Jennie Bannon traveled north from Brooklyn as the cook for one of Stockbridge's wealthy summer cottagers. Her wild lifestyle and taste for liquor put Jennie in the same company with Tom. They married in the autumn countryside during late September 1878.

Nine months later, the first of Tom and Jennie Kinsella's seven children were born, twin boys named James and Thomas. Big Tom supported his family as a quarryman, helping construct local roads, bridges and the summer cottages so desired by the Gilded Age elite living in Boston and New York.

Misfortune soon crushed Tom like the quarry rock stone he pulverized. Kinsella family genealogist Kimberly Kinsella documents a host of tragedies dogging her ancestor beginning in 1883. Tom's fourth child, a baby boy, died at birth on New Year's Eve that year. Perhaps it's just a coincidence that future crimes masterminded by Tom occurred around this season. Anniversaries certainly must have had an impact on Big Tom. While incarcerated at Wethersfield State Prison under the alias of Joseph Corbett, he gave his birth date as April 1865—a pivotal month in American history, marking the end of the bloody Civil War, but morosely, also the date of President Lincoln's assassination. Perhaps symbolically, "Corbett" was also the name of the soldier who shot John Wilkes Booth.

At the onset of 1885, thirteen months after the death of their baby son, the Kinsellas' twin boys, Tommy and Jimmy, age five and a half years, and their three-year-old daughter, Lizzie, all died of diphtheria. The dark cloud followed Thomas and his family. Tom's brother Andrew, his partner in stone cutting, found work at the Shadowbrook mansion. With its extensive walls and over one hundred rooms, the structure was a mason's dream job. Upon completion, Shadowbrook became the largest home in America. Sadly, Andrew Kinsella was horribly mangled and died in a dynamite explosion at the Lenox construction site in 1893.

Kimberly sadly notes, "Between December 1883 and March of 1893, Thomas lost two of his brothers, a sister-in-law, four of his children, three nieces and two nephews. It has been suggested that these losses may have precipitated a mental illness."

Attempting to shake his bad fortune, there was a period from late 1891 to early 1892 when Tom lived in Bridgeport. He rented a home on East Main Street and found work as a truck man for the Union Metallic Cartridge Company on Barnum Avenue. Some speculate that he was also employed by James Beardsley during this time. In any event, while staying in the city, he became acquainted with the old man's rumored wealth. Kinsella left the east side abruptly. He found his wife in a compromising position and attacked the man. After his arrest, he moved his family to Brooklyn, where he established the crime ring.

Following the Beardsley job, the Masked Burglars plied their trade in and around Stockbridge. Kinsella's familiarity with the summer cottagers led to nightly raids with his lieutenant, Michael Sherlock. During the summer and autumn of 1893, this realm of the rich was transformed into what the *New York Times* described as an "armed band of resistance...where streets are deserted [and] houses have been bolted and barred." Alternating between western Massachusetts, Long Island City and Bridgeport, the Masked Burglars, under the leadership of Big Tom, became the most notorious gang operating in the East.

After his capture at the Wheeler house, and subsequent years of pacing a five- by eight-foot brick cell, Kinsella remained silent about his role in planning upward of sixty successful heists. He was denied parole in 1901 but was eventually released from the state penitentiary sometime between 1906 and 1909. Kinsella returned to Massachusetts, where he picked up the trowel and resumed his former profession as a stonemason.

Decades later, according to Kimberly Kinsella, Thomas was involuntarily committed to Northampton State Hospital by his son. Eight months afterward, in June 1932, Tom Kinsella died in this psychiatric facility. In the end, Big Tom did finally escape torment among the hills of his hometown of Stockbridge, the village where so many years before neighbors had shaken their heads whenever the Kinsella brothers swaggered along Main Street. Thomas Kinsella was buried in an unmarked grave in Stockbridge's St. Joseph's Cemetery.

As for the legacy of the cattle rancher who made one of Connecticut's most beautiful parks a reality, karma caressed Bridgeport just as Big Tom walked free from Wethersfield Prison. In 1909, a life-size bronze statue of the Park City benefactor took its rightful place at the entrance of Beardsley Park. In front of a roaring crowd, amid fanfare he richly deserved, James Beardsley arrived home.

𝒢. 51

1898

Why should a wretched man, guilty, we will say, of murder, prefer to keep the dead corpse buried in his own heart, rather than fling it forth at once, and let the universe take care of it!
—*Nathaniel Hawthorne,* The Scarlet Letter, *1851*

Somewhere off in the distance, beyond the wooden bridge, the grappling hook again splashed. It had been nearly eight hours since the decapitated head was discovered. The steely claws hitting the incoming salt water were hardly visible now that it was so late this September 12, 1898 evening. But the obscene noise was clear to everyone who had assembled on both sides of the quarantined Seaview Avenue crossing.

Earlier that day, as summer vacation was all too swiftly coming to a close, three friends—James Jackson, age twelve; Stephen Kelly, twelve; and Henry Dellmuth, eight—leaped into the Yellow Mill Pond for a swim. On the way home, the boys challenged one another to a stone-throwing contest; the target was a stump poking out from the mud in the shadow of the Seaview Avenue Bridge. Aiming at the broken tree, young Jackson noticed a piece of cloth bobbing in the shallows nearby. Curious, he climbed down one of the bridge's thick wooden pylons and tried to haul the bundle ashore with a stick. "It's soft," James shouted up to his friends. "Probably a dead dog." A hard tug at the white wrapping sent Jackson screeching. He scurried back up onto the planks, where his friends questioned what was the matter. They all peered down into the shallows. A human foot was exposed. The horror-stricken boys ran to the closest house and fetched William Burr. Mr. Burr shook his head, disbelieving, but still went with the boys. Approaching the bridge, Burr saw two white bundles in the water and, looking down, was sickened to view exactly what the boys had described. Now the children ran to James Jackson's uncle, John J. Calhoun, whose house was just down the road. Uncle John attached a piece of metal to a pole and raced to the bridge just as Officer Hazel, of the Bridgeport bicycle patrol, happened to be peddling by.

The tide had retreated, so it was impossible to get a boat to the spot. Officer Hazel lay prone on the planks, stretching the rude hook, and carefully fished the bundle out of the mire. The wrapping had already begun to fall away, revealing both lower limbs of a woman. The legs had been cut in two at the thighs and again just above the knees. They were carefully bound in what looked like a white tablecloth but was in reality a kind of thin rubber material. A rock had been used to sink the severed parts. A crowd of curiosity-seekers began to assemble. One spectator commented aloud that the slicing job was so clean it must have been accomplished by a butcher or a doctor. The second bundle was more difficult to raise. A small boy was selected from the group of onlookers and lowered by rope to the cloth. When he couldn't budge the mysterious package, the boy was given a knife to cut away the rope that weighed the package down with a stone. The boy and bundle were hoisted up to the floor of the bridge. The stone anchor slipped from his grasp, splashed back into the tidal puddles and was retrieved. Up on the wooden span, the crowd pressed in for a better gander at the soaking parcel at Officer Hazel's feet. The knots were loosened. The policeman gagged in terror. The head of a woman, her long brown hair surreally braided with a piece of cotton cord, rolled onto the planks.

All afternoon, the police and hundreds of volunteers scoured the oozing mud flats of the Yellow Mill Pond. When the tide finally came in, mud-crusted waders were exchanged for the grappling hook. The reeking mud absorbed the morose clanging with a vicious slurping sound, like a hissing creature roiling in a nightmare. The Bridgeport police officers had doffed their blue coats and dome-shaped hats. It was easier this way to swing the rope and hook through the air above their heads. The soaked cord was dragged through the seven-foot-deep salt water once more before being raised, thoroughly dripping, up to the bridge railing. Nothing was attached. Squinting into the swirling tide, the officer watched the waters from Long Island Sound surge beneath the bridge. Frustrated with the nonproductive search, Officers Hall and Larkin returned to headquarters. But they were

The Seaview Avenue Bridge once crossed an arm of the Yellow Mill Pond. These wooden planks witnessed a horrible scene that shocked New England. *Courtesy of the Connecticut State Library.*

also silently relieved. Tonight, the Yellow Mill Pond would not yield any more body parts.

Ghosts and sea serpents had long been said to haunt Bridgeport's Yellow Mill Pond. But nothing so horrific had ever shocked the city, and indeed all of Connecticut, as the discovery of this woman's dismembered body at the Seaview Avenue Bridge.

Not to be confused with the Yellow Mill Bridge farther south, the Seaview Avenue Bridge was slow to come into existence. As early as 1880, West Stratford's citizens clamored for a more direct route across the wide stub of an arm on the pond's east side, extending Seaview Avenue above Connecticut Avenue, thus connecting the area with the harbor. By decade's conclusion, West Stratford was annexed by Bridgeport, becoming the city's East End, and the six-hundred-foot-long, twenty-foot-wide Seaview Avenue Bridge was christened. The bridge is now long gone and the wide tidal inlet filled; even the portion of September pond bank that silently witnessed the body being tossed from the wooden bridge now rests under countless tons of a gravel company's landfill.

At seven o'clock on the evening the head and legs were pulled from the pond, the remains were brought to John Cullinan's morgue downtown, where a morbid throng had gathered. Word of the crime had spread, and people flocked for a glimpse of the head. The police used the opportunity to help identify the victim. Anyone wishing to view the unknown girl was asked to form a single line and proceed from the Union Street door and exit onto Main Street. About 2,500 people marched through the undertaker's that night. The next day, that number increased to nearly 6,000. Many thought they'd seen the attractive blue-eyed face somewhere, but no one could say for certain. One of the policemen examining the cloth used to wrap the head noticed a peculiar marking: "G. 51." It was written in indelible ink on the left leg waistband of a man's size 34 undergarment.

Early the following morning, two men crossing the Seaview Avenue Bridge on their way to work discerned another bundle in the water. Securing a boat, they rowed out roughly twenty-five feet from the bridge to where the package had been tossed with some force. They were surprised to locate an additional sack under the crossing. When opened, the bundle revealed the trunk of a woman that had been adroitly carved in half. The heart and lungs were intact, but all the other organs were missing. Again, the remains had been stowed with a rock and wrapped in a long rubber sheathing. It was impossible for so many eyes to have overlooked the large bundle during the previous day's search. Whoever committed the crime had daringly returned to the Seaview Avenue Bridge and disposed of the remaining body parts.

Doctors and the police examining the body parts determined the woman had stood roughly five feet, four inches, and weighed approximately 110 pounds. She had long, fine, brown-red hair and blue eyes. Any thoughts of "Jane Doe" being a prostitute were dismissed; her nails had been recently manicured, and her teeth and fingers were free from tobacco stains, a sign in those days of the "street class." Although most of the internal organs were missing, authorities were confident that death had resulted from an abortion that had gone terribly wrong.

For days, the morose parade continued to plod through the undertaker's door. Children were expressly forbidden to enter the rear room of the morgue where "it" was. Family members, boyfriends and friends from across the Northeast sadly seeking their missing loved ones took the sigh-filled journey to Bridgeport. The head was retained, floating in a wooden bucket filled with embalming fluid. For those uneasy about the prospect of viewing the actual head, photographs were taken and offered, both full-face and profile, prior to entering the morgue's backroom. Many visitors left ashen-faced and sobbing; they felt sure they recognized the woman.

Immediately, the victim was said to be a girl who worked on Main Street at Howland's store, but she was alive and well in Stratford. Then a man was certain she was a nurse from Bridgeport, but she too was among the living. Then a second nurse was thought to be the dead woman, but she was visiting

Many people thought they had seen her before. The head of the unidentified woman was placed in a bucket filled with embalming fluid and stored in the backroom of a morgue. *Courtesy of the Connecticut State Library.*

New Milford. A woman from Norwalk; an Ansonia girl someone met at a Labor Day picnic; a Mount Holyoke student who'd vanished the previous autumn; a Poughkeepsie resident—every hour the list of possible victims expanded. But when each person turned up alive, the police were left only more frustrated.

On September 15, a stranger arrived from Middleborough, Massachusetts, and made his way through the crowd outside Cullinan's mortuary. The man requested to see the photo and then reluctantly walked to the bucket waiting in back. He brushed the girl's hair from the side of her face. "Poor Marion," he whispered. The visitor was the young woman's father, Frank Perkins. The scar he was so afraid he'd find was plainly visible at the hairline, as was a small chickenpox mark over the left eye. This was obviously Marion Grace Perkins, who had been missing from home for the previous three weeks. The next day, the Perkins family dentist telephoned the undertaker; over the phone, they detailed the number of fillings and two missing back teeth on the lower jaw. Arrangements were made to bring Marion home to Middleborough. Still, something about Mr. Perkins's claims bothered coroner Charles A. Doten, Bridgeport police superintendent Eugene Birmingham and Detective George Arnold. But after the official inquest on September 17, the body was released with a death certificate into the custody of Marion's father, and the casket was loaded on the 2:20 p.m. train out of the city. When Perkins arrived at the Massachusetts depot, he was astounded by the crowd there to greet him. Crazed by the news they provided, the bereaved father learned that his daughter Marion was actually waiting, very much alive, at their home. She had merely been away on holiday with her gentleman. The mystery returned to Bridgeport with the body: who was the dead girl?

Medical investigators figured the woman had been killed in Bridgeport either Saturday, September 10, or Sunday, September 11. The individual had been dead only a handful of hours before being placed in the pond. Some postulated that this was the work of a student's underground scientific autopsy, but that theory was abandoned since the cuts to the body did not lend to an examination. Plus, everyone noted the experienced precision of the saw. With authorities believing that the unknown girl had died as a result of an illegal abortion, suspicion was thrust on a woman committing the crime because the procedure was usually performed by a midwife.

Detectives gathered clues. Deducing that the body parts had been transported to the Seaview Avenue Bridge by carriage, the police visited every livery stable in the city trying to track down who may have rented a carriage or wagon on the evenings in question. The stones weighing down the bundles were collected and scrutinized. But the most tantalizing clue was the "G. 51" mark found on one of the garments used to wrap the decapitated head. It was considered to be a laundry mark employed to identify specific customers.

Bridgeport police questioned the owners of every laundry in the city and then visited those businesses in New Haven. Checking their ledgers, three laundries in New Haven said the mark was assigned to Henry Gill, a doctor in his mid-fifties who lived on Chapel Street. Dr. Gill was presently serving time in state prison for performing an abortion that resulted in the death of a young lady. Evidence thus began pointing to his wife, Dr. Nancy Guilford.

Nancy Alice Guilford had been implicated with her husband in the crime that sent him to jail, but she jumped bail and left the state. The midwife had reappeared and established a medical practice in Bridgeport directly across from the South Congregational Church, at 51 Gilbert Street; today the little lane is known as Cesar Batalla Way. (The Guilford place is gone, as is the house of worship, but the brick outline of the towering church is still visible on the outside wall of the Court Exchange Building.)

New England girls went missing or turned up dead whenever Nancy Guilford was around. She was pursued from Bridgeport across two continents and an ocean before being captured in London. *Courtesy of the Connecticut State Library.*

Her Park City patients didn't know Guilford had served one year in a Massachusetts prison in 1886 for an abortion during which a Lynn girl perished. Also in 1896, New Haven police hauled Guilford out of her Bridgeport office for performing a criminal abortion two years earlier. More recently, just a year before the body parts and head were pulled from the Yellow Mill Pond, she'd been questioned about the mysterious disappearance of a Wallingford girl said to have visited her office here in Bridgeport. At the time, newspaper ads publicized that Dr. Guilford "makes diseases of Women a specialty. Ladies suffering from any difficulty, incident of the sex, can consult Dr. Guilford in the strictest confidence."

A day after the body parts were found in Yellow Mill Pond, Guilford closed her house, dismissed the servants and departed for parts unknown with her daughter Eudora. Police searched the abandoned Gilbert Street residence and discovered in the furnace the charred remains of a woman's heel, the remnants of a pocketbook and corset fasteners. In New Haven, Dr. Guilford's hunchback son, Harry (a sailing master employed onboard James Parish's steam yacht, *Ceres*), innocently disclosed to newspapermen that his collar and cuffs bore the "G. 51" laundry mark.

On Wednesday, September 21, Southington, Connecticut resident Henry Gill Jr. took the long, sad train to Bridgeport. It was a macabre irony that his family shared the same last name with Dr. Guilford's incarcerated husband, but they were not related in any way. Young Henry was being sent to the Park City at the behest of his family to look at the severed female head. Henry Jr.'s twenty-six-year-old sister, Emma, had been unaccounted for since the first week of September. He entered police headquarters with a photograph of the lost sibling. Before a word was uttered, the desk captain gasped at how much the man standing before him resembled the unknown woman. Superintendent Birmingham, along with a New Haven and Bridgeport detective, walked to the morgue. Henry described a mole on the left side of his sister's neck; it had gone previously unnoticed, as the cut that had severed the head from the body bisected the mole. The head, now preserved in a jar with a plaster cast seal, was examined, and the mole became apparent. The following afternoon, Emma Gill's father, Henry Sr.; three brothers; a brother-in-law; and four friends were escorted by police to the morgue. The second identification inquest held by coroner Doten was undeniable; the dead woman was indeed Emma Gill of Southington. She'd left her job as a domestic, requesting an absence from her position due to illness. She told her family that she would be staying in Stratford with the sister of her fiancé, Walter Foster. Emma explained to her family and employer that she'd been ill and all she needed was a good rest near salt air. In reality, she'd been discreetly sent to Bridgeport by a secret lover who was not Walter Foster.

From cellar to attic, the Guilfords' home was repeatedly searched. Nosing around the backyard rubbish heap, a New York reporter uncovered an envelope sent from the Adams Express Company in Plantsville, Connecticut, to Dr. Nancy Guilford. The state's attorney acquired a warrant, and the books of the telegraph company were opened, illustrating that a popular news store clerk, twenty-five-year-old Harry Oxley from Southington, had been sending payments to the doctor before Emma vanished. Detective Arnold found another letter stating, "Send money by express." It was signed by Harry Oxley. Another bit of paper included the names Oxley and Guernsey and the word "Southington." Oxley and Howard Guernsey—a close friend of Oxley's—were both well known and from affluent families. They were pounded with questions from Bridgeport and Hartford police.

Oxley at first denied any knowledge of the crime but soon confessed that he had impregnated Emma Gill. Guernsey had loaned him the money for the abortion. The police also had others under surveillance at this time. Guilford's service staff—Rosa Drayton, a washerwoman, and her daughter Clara, a maid—were later implicated in the murder. Emma Gill's lover, Oxley, stated that Rosa had traveled to Southington to request his presence in Bridgeport as the poor girl lay dying; he did not comply. Evidence shows that Eudora Guilford wrote a letter to Rosa telling her to "keep her mouth shut" about some undisclosed matter. On September 23, less than two weeks after the mutilated body of Emma Gill was dredged from its watery grave, these four individuals were placed under arrest. Now only Nancy Guilford had to be brought to justice.

From the moment Emma's remains were first pried from the muck, the Bridgeport police had vigorously pursued clues. Just hours after the head was found in the pond, police superintendent Birmingham, with Detectives Arnold and Cronan, drove out to the remote Bishop Avenue stone quarry near Connecticut Avenue. They inspected the rocks used to weigh down the body parts and confirmed that the heavy gray mica had originated from this establishment. Two days later, while a detective surveyed local stables, the owner of the Banks Brothers livery stated that a carriage had been let out to Dr. Guilford on both nights in question. A close inspection of the conveyance she borrowed revealed stone flakes in the back of the carriage; they matched the mica samples taken from the quarry.

Nancy Guilford had been a person of interest from the very beginning. After fleeing Bridgeport, she and her daughter Eudora were trailed to Wellsburg, New York, where they stayed a few days with the doctor's brother. The Bridgeport police had continual communication with police across the Northeast by telegraph. From Elmira, New York, Guilford traveled to Albany and then crossed the border and journeyed to Montreal. Undercover Canadian authorities joined her when she set sail on the ship *Vancouver* bound for Liverpool. Members of Scotland Yard disguised as steamboat officials in England verified that the doctor traveled under the alias Mrs. Catherine Wilbur of Los Angeles, while the name tags on her luggage were "Gill," "Guilford" and "Gifford."

Quickly continuing her desperate flight from the police, Guilford departed for London by train. Arriving at the depot, she dashed to a horse-drawn taxi. Reporters were in waiting, and upon glimpsing the lady in black, the men leaped into two other carriages. A third taxi held a British detective. The chase was on. Up and down London's cobblestone streets the horses raced. At a busy intersection, the undercover man's ride was halted by the raised hand of a crossing guard, but the journalists maintained a bead on the doctor. Finally, ordering her cab to stop, Guilford climbed down from her seat and walked back to the reporters' taxis. Since there was no warrant for her arrest, and she professed only her alias, the doctor knew the scribes' actions amounted to stalking. She demanded that they cease following her or she would be compelled to speak with a constable. The newspapermen ignored her demand and continued their chase; Guilford made her threat real and did attract the attention of an officer. That pause was all she needed to tear down a narrow side lane and lose her pursuers. Guilford eventually escaped to Paris and then doubled back to London.

Relentless in their search, Scotland Yard did finally locate her in a boardinghouse on October 1. When apprehended, Guilford professed her innocence, exclaiming that her name was McAllister and she was a Chicago resident living in London for the past six months. The doctor, who was chased across two continents and an ocean, was all too well recognized. The extradition process would take a month. While strangers piled flowers high on Emma's grave, the physician was escorted back to New York aboard the steamship *Lucania* by Bridgeport detective Edward Cronan and police matron Jennie Hill. On November 19, Guilford was placed behind bars in the Fairfield County Jail to await trial.

Testimony began in March 1899 and painted a bloody affair. The coroner found that Emma Gill's death had resulted by felonious homicide at the hands of Nancy Guilford, assisted and abetted by Harry Oxley and Rose Drayton. Second-degree murder charges were lodged against Dr. Guilford, Eudora Guilford, Harry Guilford, the washerwoman Rose Drayton and Oxley.

The defense tried to cloud matters by questioning if the dead person was truly Emma Gill. Half a year before, the victim had been erroneously identified as Grace Marion Perkins. The Perkins family dentist in Massachusetts, Dr. Woodward, unintentionally perpetuated this view. He arrived at this inaccurate conclusion by having had the teeth merely described to him over the telephone by the undertaker; Woodward did not examine the teeth in person, nor did he rely on the assistance of a Bridgeport dentist. Wishing to avoid a repetition of this error, Miss Gill's remains were released to her father only after positive comparison of Emma's actual dental chart created by her Southington dentist, Dr. E.S. Rosenbluth, and shared with a Bridgeport counterpart working with the coroner. The state's attorney still demanded positive identification beyond that provided by this long-distance communication or assurances of the grieving family, who viewed the discolored and embalming fluid-soaked head through tears. Thus, a full exam was required even after her burial, and Emma Gill's head was ordered exhumed from her upstate grave. "A murder trial hinging largely upon the expert testimony of a dentist is quite uncommon," Dr. Rosenbluth confessed. The head was removed from the metallic casket and carried to the cemetery's ramshackle tool shed. The head was steadied on a broken chair. A cork held the jaw apart while the teeth were thrice explored. Exposure to seawater and then embalming fluid had discolored the enamel, leading earlier examiners at the morgue to misidentify amalgam fillings as being cement. In the graveyard, Rosenbluth carefully recorded each tooth, filling material and the method of application. This was compared to the records at his office; surprisingly, the dentist found a notation stating that he had extracted a molar that was later filled. The matter was explained as a clerical error. Inevitably, it was the unique style of work employed upon the various teeth that proved the convincing factor; the court recognized that Emma Gill was the deceased woman.

Poor Emma Gill was sawed into sections. It was the forensic exam of a dentist that finally proved the deceased person's true identity. *Courtesy of the Connecticut State Library.*

Oxley testified that he accompanied Emma to meet Dr. Guilford at 51 Gilbert Street during late August. A fee of $150 was required for the abortion, but Harry could only pay $65 at that time. He said he'd raise the remaining money and wire it to Guilford.

The court heard, according to Oxley, how Miss Gill remained at the Guilford house for about a week following the procedure. Emma's lover had no idea she became sicker day by day until succumbing to septicemia, or blood poisoning, on Saturday, September 10. The maid, Clara Drayton, slept each night at the Guilfords' and knew Emma was in the house, but she wasn't allowed into the upstairs room where the sick girl lay. Eudora, the doctor's daughter, cared for Emma and brought her meals. Only after his girlfriend had died did Oxley receive a mysterious letter from the doctor stating that he needed to "keep mum."

The dead body remained at 51 Gilbert Street overnight. On Sunday, September 11, Dr. Guilford placed Emma Gill in the bathtub and surgically sawed and carved the body into pieces. Eudora, it was hinted, assisted with the gruesome task, while Rosa Drayton cleaned the bloody linens. The state reasoned that after the body was sliced into sections, the rented carriage was brought to the Guilford place. The body parts, now carefully wrapped in rubber medical lining and garments collected from around the house, were placed inside the back of the horse-drawn buggy. Harry Guilford rode ahead on his bicycle to the Bishop Avenue quarry and waited for his mother. There, the heavy stones were selected and secured to the bundles. The young sailor pedaled next to the Seaview Avenue Bridge and made sure the coast was clear before the doctor arrived with the tragic cargo. Harry lifted the bundles and heaved them as far as he could over the railing. Dr. Guilford returned to her home while her son biked all the way back to New Haven. The process was repeated the next night with Emma's torso. The Guilfords didn't reason that the pond was impacted by the tide's currents.

The trial came to an abrupt conclusion on April 11, 1899. One of the jurors became seriously ill and would be unable to sit in court for at least a month. The defense wanted to wait for the juror's return, but the judge decreed to dismiss the jury and empanel a new one. Instead, when court resumed that afternoon, state attorney Samuel Fessenden announced that the accused desired, with the court's consent, to change her plea to guilty of manslaughter. Judge Wheeler sentenced Guilford to a fine of one dollar and a term of ten years in the state penitentiary.

During May of that same year, the cases against the remaining defendants—Harry and Eudora Guilford, Rose Drayton and Harry Oxley—were dismissed, some said in accordance with a deal cut by the state and the defense. With good behavior, Dr. Guilford was freed after an eight-year stint. It's strange to consider that Nancy Guilford, who was placed behind bars in part due to the evidence of the "G. 51" lettering on her family's clothing, spent nearly a decade in the prison's garment department bent over a sewing machine.

Dr. Henry Gill, who was released from prison in 1901, parted ways with Nancy Guilford. In 1916, at the age of seventy, Henry married his forty-year-old housekeeper. It was said that he never had obtained a divorce from Nancy; in fact, he is supposed to have replied to that question that no divorce was needed, since he'd never been married to the woman. Two years later, he was arrested for performing another botched abortion.

Nancy Guilford also continued her run-ins with the law. In 1920, at age sixty-six, Guilford was practicing medicine in Hartford under the alias of Alice Gibbs. She was arrested again for conducting an abortion during which the patient died. Details concerning Nancy Guilford's own demise are sketchy. The *Directory of Deceased American Physicians* lists that she expired on December 31, 1929, but it was rumored that she'd already been dead for years.

A darkness shadowed Harry Oxley his remaining days. Two years after the trial, he became extremely ill when his lungs began to hemorrhage. He did recover and eventually marry. Later, Harry expanded his parents' news and stationery shop into a popular Southington department store. However, something sinister possessed the Oxley house. The place witnessed at least two strange and unexplained fires. In 1939, a blaze was officially deemed caused by malevolent and rare "spontaneous combustion," and another, during the fall of 1940, was reasoned away by the fire chief as originating from a spark flying out of a backyard leaf fire. A supernatural presence seemed bent on obliterating the family name. Birds were known to descend on the large Oxley store's billboard and peck away at the advertisement until the words were unreadable. Harry Oxley died in 1941.

The murky legacy of the Yellow Mill Pond persisted. During the spring of 1915, nearly twenty years after the head and body parts of Emma Gill were dredged from these waters, a steam shovel excavating the pond's eastern shore unearthed a woman's torso. The body was buried about five feet deep and had decomposed in the ground for about a year. It's not known if the person's identity was ever learned. But newspapers were quick to note that a blue vest, found in the tangled brush nearby, had the letters "B-25" written on it.

Mad Man Blues

1915

I'm gonna come around and kick your door
I got the mad man blues
Man don't you know, don't you know
—John Lee Hooker, "Mad Man Blues"

Avon Park was a late nineteenth- and early twentieth-century neighborhood located on the Bridgeport and Stratford town line. The area had absorbed the name of a recreational spot along the railroad tracks a half mile into Stratford. Expanding the small corner "park" was the brainchild of Andrew Radel, president of the city's trolley line, the Bridgeport Traction Company. The manager was keen to establish a safe outdoor entertainment venue for children and church groups. Radel's dream came to fruition faster than a runaway streetcar. The park officially opened on June 6, 1895, with a surreal landscape of ten thousand upturned faces oohing and ahhing at a blazing two-hour pyrotechnic show. No one could have guessed that the whistling rockets and baritone explosions would be outdone twenty years later by a few seconds of gunfire. That future volley was merely the crescendo of a devil's list of misfortunes darkening the bucolic grove.

The recreational retreat lay within the much larger Avon Park district, whose boundaries informally ran from the end of Connecticut Avenue around St. Michael's Cemetery and southward to about Birdseye Street. The area was unique for several reasons. The Bridgeport portion was whimsically dubbed Carville due to residents' recycling old trolley cars and converting them into homes. The Stratford portion of Avon Park hosted the sport of kings. In 1897, a group of athletic-minded citizens acquired forty acres (stretching east from today's Honeyspot Road) and erected the Nutmeg Park horse-racing track. But the crowning jewel of the area was the picnic grove dubbed Avon Park, situated at the intersection of Stratford, Honeyspot and South Avenues.

Despite various leisure incentives and the many attempts to tame the spot, the greater Avon Park area had drawbacks. Foremost, it was a marshy site interspersed with dense thickets. Engineers were forever experiencing problems draining the land whenever building plans moved forward from blueprints. The brambled landscape took an even more forlorn appearance with its abandoned farms. Visitors couldn't quite put a finger on it, but as endearing a locale as groomed and decorated Avon Park might appear, there was something definitely strange about that picnic grove. Huge crowds came for barbeques, summer carnivals and labor gatherings, but the fact remained—no matter how magnificent the rallies, the place was, well… lonely. Sure, there was crime. As to be expected, professional pickpockets arrived from New York, targeting the balloon ascension during the park's opening week. But more so, the grove and bandstands seemed cursed. Exactly one day shy of the park's three-month anniversary, a ten-year-old boy fractured his skull and died when he was struck by a swing.

Avon Park's enthusiastic boast that it offered nighttimes "brilliantly illuminated with electric lights" became hubris in the sunken eyes of that "something" slithering out from the region's drained swamps. Murder became part of Avon Park history, too. Plus, there was a mysterious fire at nearby Nutmeg Park right after the racetrack opened; buildings, stables and several horses were destroyed.

However, the year 1915 marked an especially sinister grip on the grove. Accidents plagued the area. Car crashes and fires claimed lives. An eccentric recluse was found dead inside his Avon Park hut. Body parts were turning up again not too far away near the Yellow Mill Pond.

Europe's war, which had ignited the summer before, had an incredible impact on Bridgeport. The "Essen of America" supplied weapons to belligerents as factories and fortunes exploded across the city. By this time, the half-mile racetrack at Avon Park had been rented by industrialist Christopher J. Lake and his Aero Company, manufacturers of even-keel aeroplanes and airborne motorboats. The racecourse occupants changed hands again during June 1915, when a group of professional racers leased part of the park with hopes of converting it into a speedway for motorcycles and automobiles. The Fourth of July grand opening was derailed by inclement weather. When the very first motorcycles took to the oval a week later, races had to be curtailed due to terrible crashes.

Tired of the relentless financial drain, in late 1915, the Bridgeport Traction Company finally sold the park to developers. The $20,000 price tag included a number of acres, minus the trolley barns on the grove's Stratford Avenue boundary. A part of New England's Victorian summer memories was erased when the old dance halls, refreshment booths, bandstands, balloon grounds and acrobatic stanchions were leveled. Housing was needed for the ever-increasing number of immigrants summoned to sweat in Bridgeport's munitions factories.

However, the anticipated boom in this area did not materialize. Try as they might, engineers once again could never properly drain the district's marshes. Hardscrabble farms remained. Fields returned to overgrown thickets, disguising abandoned buildings and barns. Worse yet, bluebloods frowned on the ethnically segregated enclave locating here. Prejudiced folks contemptuously viewed the rough-and-tumble neighborhood as fitting only for America's most recent arrivals—Italians.

Even with its legacy of fatal accidents and failed racetracks, Avon Park was about to take a darker turn. The name Lyndel V. Bosworth may not have the harsh clang of a coldblooded gangster locked in its syllables, but this young man from Providence, Rhode Island, crammed a lifetime of ill will into a few short years.

Lyndel was born in 1895 into a working-class family. His dad was a machinist employed in a wheel factory, and his older brother, Harold, was a draftsman for an architectural firm. They were not necessarily wealthy, but the Bosworth clan was certainly getting along okay. Yet despite his family's hardworking background, Lyndel would have nothing to do with earning a daily wage. The boy had a tough life, especially when other children made fun of him. He'd suffered an accident when he was six months old. It left Lyndel's right arm a shriveled appendage, his forearm paralyzed and his wrist badly twisted. Family members blamed the boy's antisocial disposition on this handicap and a supposed clot he had in his brain. Lyndel's response was to thrust his crippled hand deeper into his pockets and sneer at the world. Just out of school, eighteen-year-old Lyndel got a good job as a teller in a Cranston, Rhode Island bank. The promising young clerk's business future was dashed when one day he walked out the door with a typewriter. Lyndel embraced his newfound path of thievery. Traveling throughout New

England, he established a rap sheet in every major city. The Northeast was Lyndel's oyster, and he was eager to wrench out a pearl. Apprehended on plenty of occasions, he was always released when police pitied his handicap. Finally, this string of goodwill ended when he landed in a Toronto prison for larceny.

After almost a year in the slammer, Bosworth returned to his hometown, Providence. He kicked around Rhode Island's capital city looking for employment, even seeking serious recommendation for a job in one of Bridgeport's munitions factories. While waiting for a response from the plant, he rolled a Providence fruit peddler for the fun of it. Bosworth reeled in nineteen dollars. With job prospects remaining nil, the ex-con headed southward, resuming his thug-like ways.

Around Labor Day 1915, Bosworth robbed several businesses in New Jersey, netting cash, clothes from a haberdashery and a prized .32 Savage semiautomatic pistol. The "live fast, die stupid" mentality got chiseled deeper into Bosworth's head. Traveling back north, Bosworth cased jobs in Rhode Island and along the eastern Connecticut shore. Around this time, Bosworth got to using the gangster alias "Honey Budlong" and hooked up with another petty hood, John McNally.

The pair entered a New Haven market in mid-October 1915 and forced the butcher to pose animal cracker–style inside his walk-in freezer, long enough for the crooks to remove cabbage from the register. Two weeks later, Bosworth leaned into an open sedan and strolled off with some good-quality buffalo fur carpets. It was getting to be that time of year when car passengers needed a blanket; Bosworth smiled thinking about the owner shivering in the breeze.

Attempting to unload the rugs at Palmer's Garage on Crown Street in New Haven, the repairman realized a fix was on. Palmer played dumb—"Come back later today and I'll give you my decision"—and then immediately rang the cops. McNally was busted at the garage when he returned that morning. At the same time, Detective Bennett W. Dorman left headquarters aboard a trolley, only to find Bosworth on the corner of Crown and Park with the two plush robes draped over his arm. Unaware, the young criminal waited for his partner, anticipating easy greenbacks. A struggle between Bosworth and the cop ensued. Witnesses turned toward the sound of the single pistol shot and saw Dorman bleeding in a pile of brown leaves in the gutter. A passing truck driver raced the detective to the hospital; recovery didn't seem likely.

Telegraph wires carried an all-points bulletin to every police station across the Northeast. Newspapers ran descriptions of the desperado: "Lyndel V.

Bosworth, goes by the alias Honey Budland or Budlong. 21 years of age. 5 feet 7 inches, medium build; smooth shaven; CRIPPLED RIGHT HAND; usually wears his collar up." New Haven police were certain Bosworth remained nearby, lurking somewhere in the city. In reality, he had worked up a serious sweat hoofing the rails down to familiar territory—Bridgeport.

Just hours after the shooting, sixteen-year-old James Buckley and eighteen-year-old George Bifield sauntered with their newfound friend over to Lucksinger's Diner near the junction of Stratford and Connecticut Avenues. Mooching a bite to eat, Bosworth cozied with the two naïve East End juveniles, who were enthralled with his tales of street bravado.

Bosworth explained that he was an out-of-work bookkeeper. The boys asked, "Why don't you get a job in one of the city's arms works? There's plenty of them."

Bosworth raised his withered right arm: "Sure. How d'ya suppose I'd get hired with this?"

The jailbird was concealing his morning's résumé, but the day's papers had already hit newsstands with a front-page description of him. The two teens had a clear idea of who they were dealing with. When the crew hooked up again that evening, one of the teens produced a copy of the *Bridgeport Evening Farmer*. The coverage of the Dorman shooting pushed Bosworth into a rage. "Don't show me that," he shouted. "For God's sake, don't show me that. Don't mention it. I'm the guy that shot him." Bosworth vowed he'd hunt down and kill the teens if they ratted on him.

Calming down, Bosworth proffered that the youngsters join him in a crime wave. Shekels could be easily harvested once transportation was arranged. The plan was on: rob Lucksinger's restaurant, Clancy Brother's Saloon and Wolff's deli. To ensure they'd never have to pause at a filling station, the gang would steal a week's worth of gasoline from the local Gulf Refining Company and peel away in an auto heisted from Moore's Garage on Union Avenue. The three would drive to New York City, "the best place in the world to hide," grinned Bosworth. Two days later, Monday night, the scheme would be implemented. For the teenagers, frightened as they were with the gunman, it was great fun playing gangster.

After wrestling with the New Haven cop, escaping to Bridgeport and now outlining his criminal strategy, Bosworth needed to grab some rest. Buckley and Bifield recalled an abandoned barn nearby—the perfect hideaway. There was one drawback, however. The two young men glanced at each other before turning to Bosworth. "It's haunted," the boys murmured.

Always the tough guy, Bosworth shrugged his shoulders. "Ghosts! Let's see who's scared of what when I'm unloading my .32 into 'em."

That evening, Lyndel Bosworth was escorted into the overgrown fields behind the trolley company's garages on the corner of Surf and Stratford Avenues. Pressing aside vines and thorns, the gang of three uncovered the ramshackle Spada barn. The warped wooden structure loomed in every local child's nightmares. No one was really sure how the place ever garnished its shunned legacy; it was just one of those strange denizens of Avon Park. Lending to the ghostly atmosphere, the old barn stood in the woods directly across the street from St. Michael's Cemetery.

The unused building was far enough away from Avon Street, and the Spada house, that Bosworth's presence wouldn't be detected. "This place is a natch," he observed. "Excellent spot to grab some sleep."

As night crept over Avon Park, Bosworth peered from the hayloft door opening onto the desolate landscape. "Finally, everything is jazzing for me," he smiled. "Even a sniper's roost for any coppers sniffing 'round."

The Avon Park neighborhood and the woods surrounding the haunted barn where Lyndel Bosworth made his last stand. *Courtesy of Stratford Public Works, Engineering Division, Town Hall, Stratford, Connecticut.*

His two young co-conspirators watched Bosworth as the shadows gathered around him. In a sad, philosophical tone, the criminal whispered, "If the bulls come, I'll get them, or they'll get me. That's all." He stretched his arms and yawned. "You guys better head home and come back tomorrow."

Bifield and Buckley paused. Shrugging, they meekly said, "We're busy with stuff tomorrow."

"What kinda stuff?" quizzed the gangster.

The boys responded, "You know, a party. Tomorrow's Halloween."

"Damn Halloween to hell," Bosworth wailed. "You show up here so we can discuss them robberies."

That last day of October, Bosworth boldly strolled the streets of Bridgeport, with not a care in the world about being found. The boys showed up as he had demanded, and Bosworth expounded on the crimes they'd planned. Now the teens were in a jam. Hours were counting down to the robberies. They did not want to follow this unbalanced criminal, but they were sure he'd come gunning for them if they balked. Their decision was finalized early Monday, November 1, 1915, when word reached Bridgeport from the New Haven hospital of Detective Dorman's death. Lyndel Bosworth was a murderer. Bifield and Buckley knew they could be held as accessories if they went along with him for the ride.

The teenagers consulted old-timers they trusted at Clancy's Saloon. Wide-eyed, the grizzled barflies demanded that the boys drop a nickel and ring the New Haven blue shirts. The teens called immediately from the bar, informing police that Bosworth was holed up in the "haunted barn in Avon Park." The New Haven police ordered Bifield and Buckley to stay where they were and contact the Bridgeport authorities. The local police met the teens, and the group drove over to the corner of Stratford and Surf Avenues. The New Haven police made record time arriving at the spot. One of the Bridgeport patrolmen excused himself, went to a gun shop on Fairfield Avenue and borrowed a high-powered rifle, along with two pockets full of soft-nosed bullets. Returning the rifle was never a question; the bullets, on the other hand, were bought and paid for.

A plan came together quickly. At first, the teens were reluctant to confront the mad man again, but being reminded of their implications in a cop slaying convinced them to enter the barn. Bifield and Buckley roused Bosworth from sleep; he spun out of the hay with his gun leveled at the boys. Realizing who it was, his only friends on earth, he lowered the pistol, smirking, "You better be more careful, I coulda plugged you both. This Savage is the best weapon for our work. I'll have to get one for you."

"Hon," the boys panted, "the cops got word. They're searching every barn in Stratford."

Bosworth anxiously peered out the loft door. "What'll I do to escape?"

Buckley and Bifield told Bosworth he'd better get to the train tracks on the other side of Stratford Avenue and jump a freight out of town. The police trap was coming into fine form.

Bosworth, considering his predicament, snickered, "They'll never take me alive," and ran from the weathered barn. He raced for the tin trolley sheds lining the road; from there, all he'd have to do was cross the street where the rails, and freedom, waited. In a jog, Bosworth emerged from the woods while transferring his black-handled .32 from an inside vest pocket to his belt for easier access, when the police shouted for him to halt. Instead, Bosworth ran. Groping for his pistol, he turned to fire as smoke from the police volley filled the field behind the trolley barns. A numbing pain rippled across his lower body. He'd been hit. Sprawled across the ground, Bosworth reached for his weapon. Pushing up on his paralyzed arm, he twisted his body, attempting to fire, but officers stepped on his wrist and removed the pistol from his grip.

Lyndel Bosworth was raced to the emergency hospital at Bridgeport police headquarters and then operated on at St. Vincent's Hospital. It was all in vain. The sole bullet that struck him from behind was wedged inoperably near his abdomen. The twenty-one-year-old regained consciousness long enough to talk with police and nursing staff. He was curious whether he had been hit by a shotgun blast or a slug. Bosworth realized that if he survived he'd be fitted for a noose. Still singing the mad man blues, he knew his journeys on earth were not quite through. Lyndel Bosworth's final raspy words were, "When I croak, ship my carcass to Providence, Rhode Island."

One has to wonder. On late October nights, when the wind crosses today's paved lots and vanished fields of old Avon Park, do the sounds of invisible children at play mingle with the pounding hooves of a long-gone Nutmeg racetrack? Were those distant pops and bangs that just sounded merely neighborhood fireworks, or were they the ghostly echoes from a long-ago shootout at the haunted barn?

Sources

ARTICLES

Bell, A.N., ed. "A Very Striking Case..." *The Sanitarian: A Monthly Magazine Devoted to the Preservation of Health, Mental and Physical Culture* (December 1878): 553–54.

"The Bridgeport Tragedy—Particulars of the Murder of Captain Colvocoresses—Large Insurance Upon His Life, With List of Companies Interested." *United States Insurance Gazette and Magazine* (June 1872): 104–5.

"Captain Kidd's Treasure." *American Journal of Numismatics* (October 1889): 41–42.

Colvocoresses, Harold. "Captain George Musalas Colvocoresses, U.S.N." *Washington Historical Quarterly* (July 1934): 163–70.

Dwyer, John B. "Observations from the Edge of the World." *Naval History Magazine* (June 2008): 52–57.

"Galvanic Experiments on the Dead." *Frank Leslie's Illustrated Newspaper*, December 29, 1866.

Porter, Dr. George Loring. "How Booth's Body Was Hidden: The True Story Told for the First Time in the Columbian, The Army Officer Who Hid the Body Relates the Grewsome [*sic*] Details." *Columbian Magazine* (April 1911): 64–82.

———. Letter to the Editor. "J. Wilkes Booth: Dr. Porter Present When Murderer's Body Was Secreted." *New York Times*, April 4, 1909.

———. "Recognition of Death." *Boston Medical and Surgical Journal* (June 29, 1882): 615.

———. "Signs of Death." *New York Medical Eclectic* (September 1882): 27–29.

Rogers, Frederick T., MD, ed. "Malpractice Suit in Bridgeport." *Atlantic Medical Weekly* (April 4, 1896): 219–20.

Rosenbluth, E.S., DDS. "A Legal Identification." *Dental Cosmos* (October 1902): 1029–34.

Sterling, Julian H. "Bridgeport—A Story of Progress (Part I)." *Connecticut Magazine* 8 (1903–4): 785–802.

BOOKS

Bonner, Willard Hallam. *Pirate Laureate: The Life & Legends of Captain Kidd*. New Brunswick, NJ: Rutgers University Press, 1947.

Bridgeport City Directories, 1865–1927.

Chapman, Gerard. *The Gentleman Burglar and Other Favorites*. Great Barrington, MA: Attic Revivals Press, 1994.

Colvocoresses, George Partridge. "A Sketch of the Colvocoresses-Calvocoressi Family, Written On Board the U.S.S. Lexington at Port Royal, South Carolina, A.D. 1902." Unpublished manuscript, Litchfield Historical Society.

Dougan, Andy. *Raising the Dead: The Men Who Created Frankenstein*. Edinburgh, Scotland: Birlinn Limited, 2008.

Dow, George Francis, and John Henry Edmonds. *Pirates of the New England Coast, 1630–1730*. Salem, MA: Marine Research Society, 1923.

Eisenschiml, Otto. *Why Was Lincoln Murdered?* Boston: Little, Brown and Company, 1937.

Ellis, William Arba, ed. *Norwich University 1819–1911: Her History, Her Graduates, Her Roll of Honor*. Vol. 2. Montpelier, VT: Capital City Press, 1911.

Goddard, M.E., and Henry V. Partridge. *A History of Norwich, Vermont*. Hanover, NH: Dartmouth Press, 1905.

Hamilton, Allan McLane, and Lawrence Godkin. *A System of Legal Medicine*. New York: E.B. Treat, 1895.

Hinman, R.R., ed. *Letters From the English Kings and Queens Charles II, James II, William and Mary, Anne, George II, &c. to the Governors of the Colony of Connecticut, Together With the Answers Thereto, From 1635 to 1749*. Hartford, CT: John B. Eldredge, 1836.

Hudnut, James Monroe. *Semi-Centennial History of the New York Life Insurance Company, 1845–1895*. New York: New York Life Insurance Company, 1895.

Lewis, John B., and Charles C. Bombaugh. *Stratagems and Conspiracies to Defraud Life Insurance Companies: An Authentic Record of Remarkable Cases*. Baltimore, MD: James H. McClellan, 1896.

Lewis, Lloyd. *Myths After Lincoln*. New York: The Press of the Reader's Club, 1941.

Lovecraft, H.P. "Herbert West—Reanimator." *New England Ghosts*. Edited by Frank D. McSherry Jr. Nashville, TN: Rutledge Hill Press, 1990. Originally published in *Home Brew* (February–July 1922).

Mellor, Anne K. *Mary Shelly: Her Life, Her Fiction, Her Monsters.* New York: Methuen, 1988.

Orcutt, Samuel. *A History of the Old Town of Stratford and the City of Bridgeport, Connecticut.* New Haven, CT: Tuttle, Morehouse & Taylor, 1886.

Osborn, N.G., ed. *Men of Mark in Connecticut.* Vol. 3. Hartford, CT: William R. Goodspeed, 1907.

Porter, Dr. George Loring. "America's Most Famous Murder." *The Mystery Companion.* Edited by A.L. Furman. New York: Gold Label Books, 1943.

———. *Tragedy of a Nation.* Hartford, CT: Case, Lockwood & Brainard, 1900.

Porter, Mary W. *The Surgeon in Charge.* Concord, NH: Rumford Press, 1949.

Roscoe, Theodore. *The Web of Conspiracy: The Complete Story of the Men Who Murdered Abraham Lincoln.* Englewood Cliffs, NJ: Prentice-Hall, Inc., 1959.

Saxon, A.H. *P.T. Barnum: The Legend and the Man.* New York: Columbia University Press, 1989.

Schenck, Elizabeth Hubbell. *The History of Fairfield, Fairfield County, Connecticut: From the Settlement of the Town in 1639 to 1818.* Vol. 1. New York: self-published, 1889.

Snow, Edward Rowe. *Pirates and Buccaneers of the Atlantic Coast.* Boston: Yankee Publishing Company, 1944.

Southington, Connecticut City Directories, 1889–1942.

Stevenson, Robert Louis. "The Suicide Club." *The Strange Case of Dr. Jekyll and Mr. Hyde and Other Stories.* New York: Barnes & Noble Classics, 2003. Originally published in *London Magazine,* 1878.

Waldo, George Curtis. *History of Bridgeport and Vicinity.* Vol. 2. New York: S.J. Clarke Publishing Company, 1917.

Weichmann, Louis J. *A True History of the Assassination of Abraham Lincoln and of the Conspiracy of 1865.* New York: Alfred A. Knopf, 1975.

Wilcoxson, William Howard. *History of Stratford 1639–1939.* Stratford, CT: Stratford Tercentenary Commission, 1939.

Zacks, Richard. *The Pirate Hunter: The True Story of Captain Kidd.* New York: Theia Books, 2002.

FAMILY PAPERS/FILES/SCRAPBOOKS

"Barnum, P.T., 1800s–1929." Biographical Clippings. Bridgeport Public Library, Bridgeport History Center.

"Beardsley, James W." Clippings File. Bridgeport Public Library, Bridgeport History Center.

Colvocoresses Family Papers, 1870–1872. Created by Harold L. Colvocoresses, Litchfield Historical Society.

"Daughters of '76 Disturbed." Scrapbook: Cemeteries—Mountain Grove Cemetery, p. 3. Bridgeport Public Library, Bridgeport History Center.

Long Island Sound Pirates. Personal Files, Michael J. Bielawa.

Pirates of Bridgeport, Charles Island & Stratford—Captain William Kidd. Personal Files, Michael J. Bielawa.

"Porter, George Loring." Clippings File. Bridgeport Public Library, Bridgeport History Center.

GOVERNMENT DOCUMENTS

Hoadly, Charles J. *The Public Records of the Colony of Connecticut, From August 1689 to May 1706.* Hartford, CT: Case, Lockwood and Brainard, 1868.

Report of the Directors of the Connecticut State Prison to the General Assembly, January Session 1895. Hartford, CT: Case, Lockwood & Brainard Company, 1895.

Report of the Directors of the Connecticut State Prison to the Governor, For the Fiscal Year Ending September 30, 1895. Portland, CT: Edward F. Bigelow, 1895.

Special Laws of the State of Connecticut, Complied and Published By the Authority of the General Assembly. Vol. VII, *From the Year 1871 to the Year 1875, Inclusive.* "Amending the Charter of the Bridgeport and Stratfield Burying Ground Association," May 1873/Approved, July 3, 1873. Hartford, CT: Case, Lockwood & Brainard Company, 1880.

United States Federal Census, 1850–1920.

U.S. IRS Tax Assessment Lists, 1862–1918; District 4 Annual Lists, 1866; and Monthly Lists September–December 1862.

INTERVIEWS

Harry Colvocoresses, great-great-grandson of Captain George M. Colvocoresses, by Michael J. Bielawa, October 18, 2011.

Bernie Crowley, Bridgeport historian, concerning "Boston White, Notes" of Bernie Crowley written during summer 2005. Shared with Michael J. Bielawa, July 21, 2010.

Gregg Dancho, director of Connecticut's Beardsley Zoo, by Michael J. Bielawa, 1995–2011.

Franz Goldbach, Stratford historian, by Michael J. Bielawa, October 28, 1982.

Newspapers

Aberdeen Daily News
Baltimore American
Baltimore Patriot & Mercantile Advertiser
[Baltimore] Sun
Berkshire Courier
Boston Daily Globe
Boston Evening Transcript
[Bridgeport] Daily Leader
Bridgeport Daily Standard
Bridgeport Evening Farmer
Bridgeport Evening Post
Bridgeport Herald
[Bridgeport] Leader
Bridgeport Morning Telegram
Bridgeport Morning Telegram and Union
Bridgeport Morning Union
Bridgeport Post
Bridgeport Standard
Bridgeport Standard Telegram
[Bridgeport] Sunday Herald
Bridgeport Sunday Post
Bridgeport Telegram
Brooklyn Eagle
Connecticut Courant
Connecticut Post
Fort Worth Gazette
Hartford Courant
Hartford Daily Courant
Hartford Times
Hawaiian Gazette
Litchfield [CT] Republican
Los Angeles Herald

Meriden Daily Journal
Meriden Daily Republican
[Middletown, CT] Constitution
[Middletown, CT] Penny Press
[New Haven] Columbian Register
New Haven Daily Morning Journal and Courier
New Haven Evening Register
New Haven Morning News
New Orleans Daily Picayune
New York Evening World
New York Herald
New York Journal
New York Sun
New York Times
New York Tribune
Pittsburgh Post Gazette
Pittsburgh Press
Providence Daily Journal
Providence Daily Post
[Providence] Evening Bulletin
Providence Sunday Journal
Salt Lake Herald
San Francisco Bulletin
San Francisco Call
San Francisco Evening Bulletin
St. Paul Daily Globe
Times-Leader of New Haven
[Washington] Evening Times
Washington Times
Waterbury American
Waterbury Daily Republican

Websites

Kinsella, Kimberly. "The Kinsella Family of Stockbridge, Massachusetts." Updated October 29, 2004. familytreemaker.genealogy.com/users/k/i/n/Kimberly-Kinsella/index.html.
"Lordship Pirates and Privateers." www.lordshiphistory.com/PIRATE.

About the Author

Historian Michael J. Bielawa has authored several regional histories, and his essays have addressed such diverse topics as the mysterious creature of Lake Champlain, Bridgeport's crying stone statue and the bizarre disappearance of a Hartford, Connecticut minor-league baseball manager, as well as baseball symbolism in James Joyce's *Ulysses*. Bielawa has lectured on behalf of the National Endowment  for the Arts' "The Big Read" in Baton Rouge, Louisiana, and he is a moderator for the Connecticut Humanities Council's "Literature for a Lifetime" discussion series. Since the mid-1970s, Michael has conducted research and interviews and journeyed extensively throughout the Northeast in search of the unexplained. During his travels, Bielawa has uncovered secret rooms, tracked down historical vampire cults, interviewed a Massachusetts witch, searched for mythical creatures and pirate treasure, inspected haunted houses and wandered New England ghost towns. He has served as a guest curator for the Barnum Museum and as a special consultant to the Fairfield Museum and History Center.